Annica Vidales

PAPER-THIN

Dealing With Parental Betrayal

A True Story Of Sexual Abuse Survival and Reconciliation

PAPER-THIN
Dealing With Parental Betrayal

By Annica Vidales

All rights reserved. This book may not be reproduced in any form, in whole or in part (beyond the copying permitted by US Copyright Law, Section 107, "fair use" in teaching or research, Section 108, specific library copying, or in published media by reviewers in limited excerpts), without written permission from the author.

Disclaimer

We have tried to recreate events, locales, and conversations from the author's memories. To maintain anonymity, in some instances, I have changed the names of individuals and places and some identifying characteristics and details.

Cover photo by: Ema Person
Cover design by: Jean Dorff

- Dedication-

To my precious daughter Katniss, with love.
You show me the meaning of being present.
For that I'm truly blessed.

To my childhood bestie Malin, for all the golden memories and treasures that we've shared. May those giggly rides at the back of the house bus never end!

Table Of Contents

INTRO	6
HOW TO READ MY BOOK	9
PROLOGUE	15
Dear Diary 1	20
Dear Diary 2	24
Capsule Letter to myself 1	44
Dear Diary 3	46
Dear Diary 4 Friday 5th of April 2002	50
Dear Diary 5	55
Capsule Letter to myself 2	58
Capsule Letter to myself 3	65
Dear Diary 6	73
Dear Diary 7	76
Dear Diary 8	81
Capsule Letter to myself 4	86
Capsule Letter to myself 5	93

Table of Contents

Dear Diary 9	100
Dear Diary 10	105
Dear Diary 11	106
Dear Diary 12	108
Dear Diary 13	111
Poems written at ATSUB	115
What-If-Letter to Dad	136
Triggers reading	137
Triggers reading	139
Triggers reading	141
What-If-Letters to Little Brother	143
Triggers reading	146
Capsule Letter to myself 6	148
Capsule Letter to myself 7	153
What-If-Letters to Mom	159
Capsule Letter to myself 8	165
Dear Diary 14	182
Capsule Letter to Myself 9	184

PAPER-THIN

Dear Diary 15	201
EPILOGUE	212
Appendix: Info about ATSUB	223
About the Author	225
From the publisher	227

INTRO

I have always loved writing, playing with words, and expressing myself. Facing everyday life and the adversity from childhood abuse, writing became my coping mechanism.

I keep the many letters and notes in diaries that I have written to myself as a reference. It is as if I have embedded my words to let them rest while I continue my journey through life. Have I concealed my experiences? Maybe I packed my story away, told myself I had accepted it, and moved on. Life has shown me that repression doesn't work. It is only now that I have reached a turning point where I am ready to reconcile with my story and share it with others. My past is no longer a shameful tale hidden in the dark, but a new found treasure fueling me.

I have felt like a detective, wanting to comprehend what happened to me, why it happened, and why no one protected me. My quest was to gain a clearer picture of my life journey.

PAPER-THIN

I aimed to understand my timeline and the order of everything. In the past, I lost myself in my story, surrounded by chaos and struggling for change, unaware of the right strings to pull.

Psychologists have consistently reminded me throughout my healing process to breathe, engage in activities that bring me happiness to cope, and, above all, trust the process. Until now, writing this book seemed impossible. Deep down, I knew it would benefit other sexual abuse survivors, including myself.

When I first came into contact with Jean Dorff and The Empowering Story Program, I brushed off the idea of working on my story. I had finished my therapy some time ago. My dream of having a beloved daughter came true, and I found David the love of my life. Love developed into something more, replacing chaos. We are married and work from home for the company he founded. So, the pieces had fallen into place, and I enjoyed it.

Meeting Jean at this stage of my life helped to shift my mindset, for which I am grateful. He helped me realize I had lived my life in moderation. I survived and settled for a standard of living, but why not live fully and empower myself and others with my story?

Intro

To offer new insights, I invite you as a reader to embark on this exploratory journey with this book. It's a joy that you're accompanying me and I hope my story can support you on your life's journey too. That's why I'm telling it.

I also want to place a special thank you to all of you who, in one way or another, have supported me forward in life. Thanks to you, this is where I am today. Katniss, my dear beloved daughter, you upgraded my life beyond my wildest dreams and I'm grateful for all the adventures we get to experience together. David, my dear husband, companion, lover and business partner, I'm honored to share my life with you... The way I've grown through our 4 years together is unbelievable, and it thrills me to envision our future together. Thank you for all your support and patience throughout this writing process. Mom and Maria-Paz, without you two this writing process would never have been possible. Thank you!

Before we get started, I would like to say a few words about my book's structure and how to read it, to better prepare you for this story.

Welcome!

HOW TO READ MY BOOK

Perhaps you have already noticed that there are different components in the book. Here is a little explanation of them to help you navigate as you begin your reading.

Prologue

This is the only letter in this book that actually was sent. It was written to me by my mom right after I cut the cord to my family in 2011.

This Diary Belongs To Annica

As a kid I had a book called "My Friends" where my buddies could type info about themselves and their hobbies. I did too fill in that info.

I thought it would be nice to let you get acquainted with the 5 year old Annica, and the 11 year old Annica who actually are my co-writers. The diary texts in this book were written by them at that point in time, as well as all the other versions of me growing up into adulthood.

How to Read My Book

At the end of the book you'll also meet the current me, who added the narrator parts, to give you a little bit of explanation and pulled it all together. This is to give insight into the actual writing process and this book also is a healing journey for me to get to know myself better.

I'm very proud to say that I've made this dream come true. I've now published my own book and can tick that off my Bucketlist!

Timeline

After 'This Diary Belongs To Annica' you'll find my timeline in the footer of the pages. My intention is to give you glimpses of what life looked like during the different stages of my life. Throughout my life, I've been obsessed with figuring out what my timeline looks like, so somehow it felt important to include that in the book.

But if you are reading this book as a Kindle version, you'll unfortunately miss out on this in the reading experience, since a Kindle format only allows flowing texts. For you, I have instead added the timeline as a bullet point list of events in the appendix section.

PAPER-THIN

Dear Diary 1: (Date)

As I grew up, I wrote a lot of diaries as a hobby, both on my own and with friends. Those giggly girls' nights were the best!

This book is partly based on those daily/ weekly/ monthly occasions and you'll notice them being labeled 'Dear Diary' followed with a number to keep track of their order, and the date when they were written.

Capsule Letter to myself 1: To be opened at (Date) (Date written)

Besides from my diary texts, my book is equally based on the Capsule Letters that I used to write once a year around Christmas.

In those letters, I would write to my past self or that past Annica who wrote me a letter last year, commenting on my thoughts from back then and laughing about how things really turned out.

After that I would most likely tell about my present time, what had happened during that past year, and what I've gone through or experienced.

And then, to wrap things up, I would visualize my future self, asking with curiosity about different aspects of life that still were not revealed to me. I would also send my regards and best wishes to my older/wiser self with hopes for a prosperous life.

Poem at ATSUB 1: (Title) (Date)

During the book, you'll also come across a period of my life where I wrote many poems instead of diaries. During this time, I got the greatest kind of support through a foundation here in Sweden named ATSUB, which specializes in supporting the network around children who have been sexually abused, as well as the children who have been injured. You can read more about this organization in the appendix section.

What-If-Letter

As a young adult, to cope and release tension, I wrote several What-If-Letters to my family. Letters that never were meant to be sent and never did either. Writing those texts helped me from a healing point of view, as I allowed myself to acknowledge those feelings.

However, in Dear Diary 13, it's mentioned that I had the courage to hand over the letters to my parents! I asked my mom about it, if I might add those in the book as well, but she couldn't find them. Unfortunately I didn't save copies, so those letters that I gave to mom and dad are still a missing piece of my puzzle.

Triggers reading 'Alexandra's Room' I: (Date)

In the intro I shared with you that I published this book, so that it might support you on your life journey. Or perhaps you know someone that would benefit from reading my story?

I've had a book in my life that had a huge impact on my way to cope with being sexually abused as a child. And reading it has been a battle, a curse as much as from heaven sent. I really needed that book and at that point in time.

It was during the period of my life, where I soon was about to reach my turning point of seeking help, when I in a project at school would write a report about a development novel. I went to the library and found a book named 'Alexandra's Rum', written by Anna Mattsson, 1994.

How to Read My Book

Little did I know that the protagonist Alexandra, had a similar story, where an adult took advantage of her and used her for his own pleasure. I couldn't complete the assignment I was given writing that book rapport, and thanks to my mentor we could adjust and find me another assignment better suited.

Later in life I had the opportunity to revisit the book in a safe environment at ATSUB, where we together processed the book reading aloud and writing about it. These texts are presented in this book under the label 'Triggers reading 'Alexandra's Room' I: (Date)'

This was a challenging but so important experience for me and I felt so proud when we reached the last page.

Epilogue

In my wildest dreams I could not imagine myself answering to the letter mom sent me in 2011... The letter that you're now about to read in the prologue.

But here we are, 13 years later, and I've written my reply. You'll find it in the epilogue.

PROLOGUE

Letter from my mom

Sunday 30th of October 2011

Dear Annica!

I am sorry that I have let you down. I understand you are disappointed in me for not being there when you needed me. That was cowardly of me. I didn't know how to handle the situation. Your experiences have shaped you, and you have been strong in your decisions. I admire you for having the courage to stand up for what feels right to you.

I wish I had understood better, I could have done things differently.

Why didn't I let you do it when you wanted to lie with me but on the outside of the bed? I didn't want to understand. Why didn't I see it?

When you followed me to the bus stop and wanted to be with me, I sent you home. Why didn't I see it?

Prologue

You had written something on the lamppost and were sorry for scribbling. That should have given me a signal that all was not right.

What was most important was you and Johan, but I put my energy into my work. How could I be so narrow-minded?

I've thought about it and realized I'm afraid of conflict. When I told you something about someone I thought was doing something wrong, you told me to tell her. I was proud of you for being so straightforward, and as small as you were, you still had that realization.

I do not defend your father's behavior; it is a curse. I will never understand his actions towards you.

My behavior towards you cannot be undone, but I wish I could do good deeds in the future.

I am confused about how to resolve our situation. I am unhappy about losing you.

How can we find each other again? I miss you so much, my beloved child.

PAPER-THIN

I realize that your action is a difficult decision, but it is the only way for you to survive. You are a brave girl, and I am very proud of you.

I wish with all my heart that you can forgive me.

I love you so much!

Mum

*This diary belongs to
Annica, five years old...*

Jag år 1990

PAPER-THIN

This diary belongs to
Annica, 11 years old

Datum 20/8/1996
Min stjäjarnbild – Vädur

First name: Annica Maria
Family name: Nordström
Birthday: 21st of March
Zodiac Sign: Aries
Hair Color: Brown
Eye Color: Blue
Length: 147 cm
Weight: 35.5 kg

I play the Clarinet
Best I Know: Busy & Animals
Worst I Know: War & Farts
Member of: Book and Riding Club
Want To Be: Millionaire & Bigger
Favorite Food: Spaghetti Bolognese
Best Season: All & Autumn
I Fancy: -

Dear Diary 1

Tuesday 27th of February 1996, 7.10 pm

The darkness has slowly settled.

It is a half-moon tonight.

I am now standing outside on the soccer field near the school. It is quiet outside; only the traffic disturbs the silence.

Now and then, you can hear a dog's bark, but otherwise it's quiet.

I walk home alone. No one knows where I have been.

I hope to do this more often.

An idyllic place, yet crying inside

I grew up in a completely different climate than the harsh reality my daughter is growing up in today.

I was born and raised in a small town outside of Stockholm, Sweden, in the mid-80s, at probably one of the best times and places.

1990: A girl got violated & abused

PAPER-THIN

Living in the countryside near the capital wasn't a dream during my teenage years, but it was delightful as a child. It is a safe little community where everyone knows each other, more or less.

We lived in a neighborhood of terraced houses. 'Yellow Street' and 'Red Street' were parallel, with a narrow strip of forest separating them, and there were many playmates across the age range. As children, we could play on the plots, jump through water sprinklers, and play "The Can". As we grew older, we substituted the games with activities such as picking apples and running through our neighbor's yards, thrilled by the excitement of challenging the boundaries and stepping over the line, but yet harmless looking back at it.

I remember one particular time when I felt ashamed for stealing apples from a neighbor's yard. I told my mom about it, and she accompanied me to beg my apology to that family on my behalf.

Later in life, I learned that even my mom felt it strange that I reacted so strongly.

1990: by two very close relatives.

Dear Diary 1

Besides playing outside, there was this school area where we could hang out after school hours, play cards, and sometimes they offered us movie nights.

The library at the same entrance was also a good place to hang out, and I read many books growing up.

Once a week, there was an arrangement for the girls in my grade to meet for conversational and team-building activities with different topics each week. We had some afternoon tea and sandwiches as snacks after school in one of the classrooms, and I believe the boys were offered the same kind of meetings in a classroom nearby.

What helped us the most must have been the annual High School Musical production. We would volunteer and engage for hours to plan and practice the different scenes and dances.

That bounded kids from grade 6 or 7 up to grade 9, and we would take part in the areas that we most enjoyed, whether it was playing in the band, singing, performing in the dance numbers, or stepping up as actors in the prewritten plot from our teachers managing this project.

1990: She told her dad about it,

PAPER-THIN

Other than that, we mostly dragged around, longing to escape that dump.

In a neighborhood where everyone knows everyone, from preschool age to the start of high school... It's very difficult to break up and start over. Identity, status, and events become ingrained and are hard to shake off.

1990: but he didn't protect her.

Dear Diary 2

Sunday 13th of July 1997, 2.15 pm

We came home on Friday, and the mailbox was full of letters to Annci (Yes that's right... Annci is actually my Nickname)!

And you know what? Time flies! I've already finished this diary.

I experienced much from the 27th of February 1996 to the 13th of July 1997. You must agree with that.

Annica

The year was 1997, and I had just turned 12

Even though the abuse took place much earlier, it is still during the summer vacation between grade 5 and grade 6 that my story begins.

1997: The abuse didn't continue

PAPER-THIN

My school was quite small... only two ordinary classrooms with pupils in grades 1, 2 and 3 mixed. As we entered grade 4, together with classmates equally aged, we got a new teacher who also brought us English as a subject, and I had so much fun with friends.

Normally after that, as you grew older, kids would switch to another school with kids from the entire region we lived in. Still, our class would be the first one to continue our school years at the same place.... first, they would only need to rebuild the whole place with an entirely new area for pupils up to grade 9.

That's why we attended another school nearby during grade 5, only to start fresh in the new, shiny school building for grade 6.

However, several classmates continued their schooling elsewhere. Among them was a pair of siblings who had organized a farewell party in the building's event venue before they moved. The decorations, snacks, and punch were already prepared for the event.

1997: and instead they turned into,

Dear Diary 2

While heading there, we stopped at our local little store to grab some extra snacks and found humor in a new newspaper headline. The journalist had visited our school graduation, and our portrait with magnificent flower wreaths on our heads symbolized that the summer holidays had come to our little municipality.

I wore the same outfit as in the photo, even this evening. It comprised a round-cut short skirt and a matching belly shirt in black and white patterned fabric. The skirt felt nice against my skin when I spun.

The party was great fun, and of course, it was parent-free. Playing Truth or Dare started, but I found getting close to the boys in the class exciting. When it was my turn, I chose Truth.

On one occasion, when I challenged myself to choose Dare, I aimed to kiss one of the popular guys in the class for 30 seconds. He smelled so good, and my stomach was tingling.

I recall sitting on top of him, our lips inches apart, as his hand moved down my back and slipped inside my panties at the back.

1997: supressed memories, until...

That was the point on my timeline when everything first froze and got tangled up.

After that, things happened quickly. In shock, I rushed out of the room, and my friends pursued me home. We were all very upset and told my parents what had happened.

My father's response was straightforward and unadorned. He asked me what I wore and concluded I had to blame myself.

My mother's response was worried and upset. She called the boy's parents and emphasized what she had just learned. Scheduling a meeting at our house that weekend was the best option.

That night, after my friends left, I had difficulty sleeping.

The smirking boy

My mom, my friends, and I formed a group around our kitchen table. We cheered ourselves up, waiting for the boy and his mom to come to our house and talk about what had happened.

Dear Diary 2

His mom, appearing upset and understanding, agreed to meet us at our house because of the severe incident while on the phone.

As I shuddered, I felt nauseated in this situation. I hoped someone would apologize and show that what I had experienced was not okay.

When the doorbell rang, my mother opened the door, and the boy and his mother entered, joining us at the kitchen table. My world crashed down. The understanding woman on the phone questioned my accusation of her son groping me. Stunned, her words washed over me while the guy sat by her side, smirking. Everyone just sat there gawking, and I heard myself muttering that I must have been mistaken then…

My parents, not defending me, and the boy and his mom, portraying me as a liar in this entire situation, caused me to feel humiliated, and I hit rock bottom.

1997: up to the surface unfiltered.

I couldn't even mention this event in my diaries without feeling the painful connection. I felt humiliated because no one dared to stand up for me. Even though my mother and friends were there, I didn't feel supported. The torture persisted in the weeks that followed, with name-calling and mockery in the school corridor, all because of a rumor in the boys' circles.

That would break down any teenager. With the bottomless darkness spreading within me, this was just the start.

Please let me be buried with my legs crossed.

Strange, disgusting memories appeared in my mind soon afterward. Images like scary nightmares, but in the daytime. I quickly tried to shake off the sensations of how my father had touched my body as a little girl in a way that adults should not touch children.

It was all very confusing and disgusting. Over time, my memories came back more and more frequently and intensely. The fear made me sleep with my legs crossed, and I fantasized about writing it as a wish in my will… "Please bury me with my legs crossed."

1997: She turned to her parents but,

In the process of writing this book

It's like I get caught up in the perception of wanting to write the details as accurately as possible. What happened when?

The party... When was it?

That's not the important thing. For the sake of the narrative, I can decide on a time and let the descriptions follow the logic that follows ... but there is a notch in my writing process that hurts.

So, on Facebook, I found my friend who hosted the party and started writing messages. It would be cool if she remembered things I don't, and if it could make the picture of when the party took place clearer.

She mentions she has a vague memory of something happening, that a parent called and talked to her mom afterward.

1997: the support needed was unseen.

PAPER-THIN

As we're continuing our conversation, I'm sharing my story and that I'm in the process of writing this book, and I can hear that it touched her… with the glimpse of clarity now, since there's always felt like something strange has been going on in my home.

Growing up, her mother said something about my parents being a bit "special."

I think it's interesting because she's not the first to say something about everything being perfect, but that there's something not quite right—without being able to put a finger on it.

I experienced bullying when I was growing up … and I think it is because of that very thing that no one could pinpoint. Peers picked up on it, and it manifested itself as bullying…

Apparently, adults picked up on it, too, but remained silent.

But as an outside adult, what can you do in such a situation?

I have an inherent gut feeling that something feels a bit "off" or "weird" in that family.

1997: She was left with the feeling

In those cases, I think the most common reaction, by far, would be to look the other way and not announce that feeling.

Do you like it?

When I was little, the whole family used to sleep in Mom and Dad's double bed, although my little brother and I had our room with our beds.

We slept with them, especially on weekends when we first had a sauna in the basement and then had Friday night movies in their bedroom.

Dad would also often read us bedtime stories about exciting adventures, or we would talk about all the fun things we would do on vacation together.

After we fell asleep, Dad would continue watching movies, sitting in his leather armchair with a beer and nuts. And one beer could easily be more than that.

I was about four years old the night my dad molested me. He lay down on my side and touched my skin softly and strangely. I didn't understand why he was caressing my genitals. He asked me if I liked it.
It was stinging and uncomfortable. I felt scared, but couldn't muster the bravery to express my fear. I just wanted it to stop.

Eventually, the situation would repeat itself elsewhere.

Writers' Den

When I don't have a writing-book project, I usually keep all my diaries, letters, and calendars packed in a clear plastic box. It's said to hold 45 liters, but I'm struggling to fit more in.

Together, everything weighs 16 kg.

So it looked pretty funny when I rode my electric scooter to the writers' den, packing most of that box—a big bag balanced on my shoulder and a huge backpack on my back to carry all the "essentials"—onto the handlebars.

Dear Diary 2

So, I have borrowed my mother-in-law's apartment to dedicate myself to this writing process. She recently went to Brazil to spend Christmas and New Year with friends and left us the keys before she left. This lovely woman with several irons in the fire tends to be all over the place. So, It's a miracle that she found the keys. I wonder how many times she lost them.

When I woke up on day two here in her little studio in SoHo, the heart of Stockholm, I had already spread out a large mood board on the floor, drawn on a roll of wallpaper I found in the cupboard.

My mother-in-law has many useful items in her stash for various creative projects. Her sons would probably classify most of it as junk, but I'm grateful she had an extra roll of wallpaper for me.

My mood board is a 'wheel of life' that covers all aspects:

1998: Throughout her schoolyears...

PAPER-THIN

1. Money & Finances
2. Health & Wellbeing
3. <u>Primary relationship</u>
4. Family & Friends
5. Spiritual Development
6. Home & Surroundings
7. Fun & Leisure
8. Work & Career

As I read my journals, I realized my dreams are a pattern. I wish for control over my finances, the right energy in my wardrobe, and the pleasure and joy of wearing my clothes.

I want to have nice routines, be beautiful, radiant, and lovely, and I want to go to spa treatments and get massages.

I dream of my wedding, family, and children and long for a relationship where I feel harmony, lust, sexual liberation, love, and intimacy, but most of all, understanding, passion and playfulness.

The important thing in my story is not what the chronological timeline looked like around my romantic relationships, friends with benefits, etc... it is the party where we played Truth or Dare,

1998: coping with daily nightmares,

the period after I told my mom about the abuse, how I left home, and the move with the help of social services.

How do you ensure a reader follows along and sees the connections in your story when you are unsure of how everything is connected? Is the story logical and important?

These are the kinds of thoughts I wrestle with as I write. But one thing's for sure; I know I need to write this book.

I need this clarity and a kind of "closure" so that those dreams on my mood board can be realized.

My desire for stability is to experience peace and quiet, joy, good self-esteem, and happiness. I am proud of being ME, experiencing freedom, being free as a bird, and being genuine, authentic, and true. I jump, skip, play, am spontaneous, and am active. I have a twinkle in my eye, and I am tender, kind to myself and others, and I meet the eyes of others.

It is as if I have deprived myself of all the well-being that I deserve, that would make me sparkle and live my life to the fullest, just because I have not reconciled with my own story.

I can put aside the thought of whether the story makes sense because I know I have Jean as an editor. I rest comfortably in the confidence of his expertise and experience. My job is to allow what needs to come out to be written down and to flow freely without judgment or evaluation. The book is essential to me because it is an opportunity to release what has been stagnant within me... the knots that I have been holding so tightly and not wanting to admit. Telling my story so that it can strengthen me instead of reconciling with it... this is what gives me access to LIVE my mood board instead of longing for it.

1998: manage the facade vs breaking

Dear Diary 2

I have brought my daughter's battery-powered pillar candles and a small SPA kit that I have set up on a side table in the apartment. It's like a little candy table with goodies, face masks of various kinds, and fragrant face misters. My favorite is The Sumptuous Cleansing Butter With Calming Camomile Extract, which is great for bedtime. My Massage Melt Gel, with the scent of Eucalyptus and Rosemary, is lovely after a shower and sauna.

The last time I borrowed the apartment for a week's writing session, I visited the gym in the mornings as soon as they opened and just before their closing time. I had packed my SPA products and spoiled myself at the ladies' locker room with a well-deserved break in my writing.

This time, I'm just staying for the weekend, and instead, I'm spoiling myself with minor breaks here on site.

Last but not least, 27 diaries are carefully placed in chronological order on the window frame. They serve as both inspiration and an encyclopedia. I read them from cover to cover to find my timeline.

1998: free, along with being a teenager.

Soon to be 4, and excited about that party

I made my first note in 1989, with the help of my mother, of course, and some of my crumbling stories. I was four years old then... the same age as my daughter is now... and the same age as I was when the abuse took place. Not that you can tell from the notes themselves.

Mom has written large letters with a ballpoint pen so I can fill in the blanks with a pencil.

 "ANNICA IS GOING TO A PARTY 890114 WITH UNCLE B AND AUNTY G

GINGERBREAD HOUSE"

On that same page, I have also been practicing writing the letter B.

The sleepover that never should have been

My uncle B and his partner G had no children together, but older children from before were elsewhere.

1999: The first one she told beside

Dear Diary 2

I had a lot of fun when I went to my uncle's house, and now, as an adult, I understand they relieved my parents when I could come and stay overnight.

But then something happened that's been hard to grasp. Ever since that point in time, I have had to deal with it, understand it, and solve the riddle.

When I woke up, the room was dark, and a strange light shone through the blinds. That's how the room becomes eerily unfamiliar at night, especially when it's someone else's home, and you're just visiting. The teddy bear they lent me makes a funny humming noise when you put it on its back and set it upright. But at night, when everything is different, and mom is not around, the teddy bear's dark humming doesn't help.

When I reached my uncle's bed, he lifted the covers, and I could crawl into his arms. But I never understood why, just as my father had done. He put his hand between my legs, against my bare skin inside the nightgown. I again felt stiff, scared, and very confused.

1999: their cat, was her friend B1.

He must have heard me, right?

I proudly told my dad about the sleepover and what my uncle had done to me. I remember climbing around on our purple toilet lid while my dad changed my little brother's diaper on the changing table he had installed on the bathtub.

I loved crawling through the gap between the bathtub's edge and the changing table. It was like a perfect little hut with a sturdy roof for me.

Once, when I snuck into the hut, someone placed a mirror in the bathtub. The intended playtime unfortunately resulted in seven years of bad luck, as the saying goes, when breaking a mirror.

Changing on my little brother, my father was standing with his back to me, and he must have heard me... or?

"My uncle touched my 'cootchie' when I slept over, just as you did."...

1999: A secret too heavy for anyone

Dear Diary 2

Well, he must have heard me. His reaction was so strange. He noticed me and didn't seem as proud of me as expected. It was as if he neither wanted to hear nor confirm what I had just said.

The memories turned into suppressed memories, as the abuse did not continue but would now come back and hunt me throughout my teenage years...

1999: to bear was now dragging them,

Time capsule - Letters

I don't know what made me write letters to myself like in a time capsule...

It could be something we did in school that I then took to heart and started doing more continuously.

I remember that on our first summer vacation, we got a shoebox to take home with a yellow letter from our teacher glued on top of the lid. Our homework was to fill our box with our summer vacation to tell her and our classmates what we had experienced in the fall. I put down shells and rocks from our vacation in Denmark, the ring that rolled out of the toy machine, and a photo of us at the end of the school year.

That experience may be the starting point. Whatever it was, time capsule writing has helped me through what has felt tough. It gave me a boost to write to a future version of myself. Each time, I had forgotten what I had written and eagerly awaited the anniversary when I could open the letter and read the thoughts and greetings from the past version of Annica to my present self.

1999: both down & sabotaging health

Capsule Letter to myself 1

To be opened at Advent 2000
Thursday 6th of January 2000, 2.15 pm

Dear Annica, Merry Christmas and Happy New Year!

You absolutely must not buy more than one Christmas gift for each friend. I am not writing this to be mean to them... but it's for your good.

If you don't follow my advice, you will feel disappointed afterward. Instead, save the money for a new language trip, clothes, or maybe until you leave home.

And you... don't forget to send Christmas cards to your pen pals.

Take care, darling, and remember that beauty comes from within.

Also, how did you do on the language trip, and how is the bathroom, which I just started renovating? I hope it's ready.

2000: Peers labeled her as weird and

PAPER-THIN

How are things going on with the boy in front? Maybe it's a sensitive topic.

I hope that you have a lovely boyfriend!

I know you've struggled with friends, but I'm sure you've improved and are making great friends now.

Kisses!

2000: to cope, pen paling was joyful

Dear Diary 3

Sunday 10th of February 2002, 10.41 am

Weather: semi-clear/ humid 4°C.

Total in the bank: 1644 SEK

Clothes: gray pajamas

Feeling bored, a bit slow

Location: Mom and Dad's bed

Good things: I have wonderful friends. I always have a place to go to (B1's house). I am compassionate. I am a good listener. My birthday is coming up. I am not alone in my commute.

We were supposed to have a diary night at B1's house yesterday, but I was so tired that I arrived without you. I don't know if you can call it a depressing night, but it's worth considering.

2002: Even though they came to an at onement,

I have realized that I have repressed a lot from my life, maybe to push away all the unpleasantness. But I have deleted "all" the wonderful memories as well. Therefore, she would read glimpses of our life, and I told her not to read out about any of those unpleasant things... she promised.

But I don't think we mean the same thing. My unpleasantness is apparently not unpleasant for her.

Dealing with suppressed memories

I can feel sad even today that so many positive memories turned into suppressed memories.

It has been one of my biggest coping strategies to live my life.

It is as if I had to turn away from the majority of memories from growing up, good and bad, to be able to handle life.

I couldn't stand being with what was good... having a father who was good, nice, kind, caring, loving...

2002: it surely was liberating to start school

Because of the complexity of him also being the very worst thing that ever happened to me… that is so twisted, devastating, and the hardest thing to grasp through my therapy.

But at the same time, I'm intrigued that I already could express that I experienced suppressing memories to cope with life. Mostly, I would just hold myself up as I was holding up the facade while dealing with all what arose inside the container of being me.

Telling mom

I'm waking up on day three here in the writer's den.

I didn't sleep well last night. No matter how I turned, my back hurt, and I still feel it. I also have stiffness, compactness, and a headache.

I'm surprised by the realization that it felt exactly like that during the years when I was still living at home, before and after I told my mom about the abuse that my dad subjected me to as a child.

It took all the courage I could find inside me…

PAPER-THIN

These memories tore me during my childhood, living in this constant lie. And finally at 16, I dared to tell my mom about my father abusing me as a child.

It was the evening of my brother's birthday. I sat alone on his bed in the darkened room, my body vibrating with frustration, fear, and enormous fatigue from carrying all the horrible memories on my own. It was unbearable, so I needed my mother so badly.

She came and sat next to me on the edge of the bed, and I could hear my dad flipping through his newspaper at the kitchen table as I told her about the sexual abuse. She just sat there in shock and silence for what seemed like an eternity. I could still hear my dad turning his pages.

"Do you want us to move?" she finally asked...

"Yes, I do..."

But nothing happened...

I was at a point where I couldn't stand it any longer, and still didn't get any support from her.

2002: She had to tell mom about the

Dear Diary 4
Friday 5th of April 2002, 9.10 pm

Everything feels pointless. My whole life is in pieces at the moment, and I keep trying to tell myself that everything is just a small trifle, but it just doesn't work that way.

I wouldn't say I like Sorunda, but I don't like this house.

I don't like my family. I don't feel loved.

I think The Conservative Party says that the family is society's core and that we should invest more in it.

How will I be able to manage everything else if I don't enjoy myself and don't...?

I don't think I can handle much more. There is no place in this house that I like or that I identify with.

2002: abuse. The silence and lack

PAPER-THIN

I went to IKEA yesterday with some of my classmates. I found cozy furniture and gadgets that I would like to decorate with, but it feels unnecessary to decorate a room I wouldn't like, anyway.

I would still have to see my so-called family and have to put up with my disgusting little brother and all his stupid and mean comments. I would still have to deal with all the ugly memories.

As long as I have to stay here, forgetting everything is impossible.

The constant reminders of everything will come from everyone I meet or see and everything here in Sorunda.

I can't really explain everything because I can't really see clearly...

I am in the middle of a riot, and everything is happening simultaneously.

22nd of March 2002, is an important day.

2002: of support, made their home

Dear Diary 4

It was the beginning of Annica's new life, or at least the beginning of a new life. "The golden turning point" Thanks to Harriet, our school counselor.

It took a lot of courage for me to contact her a whole year after telling Mom without getting any support. I just waited for her to help me and help us, but everything remained silent.

Talking with Harriet made the difference.

I wonder what the social worker will say... she might deny me a new home. This place is not suitable for me if you could see how much I am suffering, you would believe me.

However, if she were to suggest a new home... I wonder what option she would recommend. Foster parents? My own little "den?" If you were to live with a family, you would feel more like a guest than at home.

But maybe you could feel loved and you wouldn't have to grow up so fast and take care of your responsibilities. I don't think I could handle that. Also, our school doesn't have a canteen. You have to bring your food; I don't think I could do that alone.

2002: an uninhabitable steam cooker.

I feel very lonely, even though I know it's not like that.

A foster family would undoubtedly change that. Dear Diary, I am afraid of the future and being left alone. I am afraid that no one will understand little me.

It hurts to read the diary I wrote in high school.

There is so much chaos that I am trying to deal with while just trying to live like a teenager and deal with all the normal teenage problems that everyone goes through.

A month passed after I told my mom and still no change, rather the situation just got worse.

I didn't talk to my family; if I needed to, I would snap at them what needed to be said. I slept poorly and suffered enormous headaches during this period.

I felt like a wet blanket when I sought help from Harriet, the school counselor. I was lucky enough to leave class once a week to see her. After a few sessions with her, they helped me contact the child and youth psychiatry and the municipality's social services.

2002.02.19: Stilnoct 5mg, 10×1

Dear Diary 4

The psychiatric doctor prescribed sleeping pills for me, as soothing music and non-prescription drugs had not helped me so far with my sleeping difficulties.

I told no one about my uncle abusing me as well. It was bad enough that my mom had to hear what my dad had done. Then, telling her that her brother had done the same thing felt overwhelming. I wanted to spare her that pain, and it wasn't like we were seeing my uncle anyway, so it wouldn't have made much difference there.

For a year, I lived in what felt like a prison or steam cooker… I started sleeping at my friends' places and…

I packed my backpack to stay at different friends' places for several days.

This was survival mode for me… managing my studies, my disgusting memories, living in this steam cooker, trying to manage a facade of being an average family, and breaking free from it at the same time with the plans of moving away from home.

2002.04.11: First meeting with Soc

Dear Diary 5

Saturday 27th of July 2002, 5.42 pm

Welcome to the beginning of Annica's new life!

Life is not a bed of roses.

It is not healthy to erase your inc written words using Tipex. It gives us the habit that it is not okay to make a mistake and that you have to correct it.

Life is full of disappointments. Just get up and try to avoid the next one.

Only some people work like you. There are a lot of jerks out there.

No one is good all the way through.

We are still in contact with Harriet, and she helped me contact BUP, The Psychologists for Children and Youths. The lady from there is Birgitta. I've only met her once, and I'm glad Harriet was there then.

2002.07.10: First meeting with BUP

Dear Diary 5

The social worker's name is Farzana, and there seems to be something wrong with her, but at least she got in touch with me after a lot of back-and-forth.

It turned out that they were looking for a new accommodation for both me and another girl. It is a so-called "youth residence," and staff will be onsite during the day.

So we would have to share a one-bedroom apartment or possibly a two-bedroom apartment. It depends.

But I am the priority. Finding out about it feels so strange. It feels like she doesn't care because she hasn't contacted me.

"This whole" summer has gone so slowly, and it feels like I'm an immigrant who hasn't been told whether I can stay here. I'm so worried I won't be able to cope with the pressure of leaving home. And then, what should I say to everyone else who is wondering? My friend M1, Grandma, and Grandpa, and my mentor Per at school, whom I will have to talk to. But he already knows that I feel bad… He looked quite worried when we had our last discussion.

2002.07.10: She suffers by being

"It's hard to leave home when you're your age... but sometimes you have no choice. If this is an extreme case."

He doesn't know how serious it is, but I'm glad he cares.

B1, Erika, and I are at M1's house, where she is home alone. I am taking care of Nisse. He is a chinchilla, and M1 does not take care of him because she is afraid of animals. Yep, so that's why I do it.

Mm... and it's pretty clear in the diary's corner *Nisse has chewed up*.

We had an excellent dinner... we had a barbecue.

Mm, yes... M1 is reading the good old diary evenings, and oh my... Kalles Kaviar! She has so much fun that she laughs her head off.

It's a shame that you write a diary less frequently nowadays *sobs* We should change that... but I'm not promising anything!!!!

B1's four-leaf clover has become a three-leaf clover *he, he*.

2002.07.10: unable to go to school

Capsule Letter to myself 2

To be opened at X-mas Eve 2002
Tuesday 6th of August 2002, 10.06 am

Hi Annica! Merry Christmas and Happy New Year!

Did you get nice Christmas presents this year, too, or was money too tight? There were probably not so many Christmas presents, but the ones you got were very nice, right?!

I'm curious to know how everything's going for you and how you feel…

I have a feeling that it will be very difficult to live alone, but you don't live alone, do you? :-)
I hope you live with a nice "roommate"- a girl who cares and takes good care of herself.

Have you done your French homework and attended every single gym class? I do not want to be mean, but I doubt it. I actually know you, remember? So I hope you won't take offense.

2002.07.10: during summer brake

PAPER-THIN

In the beginning, you were probably very enthusiastic… I know it's hard with French *hugs* But come on, girl! I know you can do it! Together, we can do wonders :-). Now, after the Christmas holidays, we take additional steps, or what do you say? *smiles nervously… a little*

Have the exchange students from France visited you yet? Last year, when they visited the previous French Class, I got so nervous that I ran away from their lesson we also were supposed to join - oops!

Shame on me! Mm… How was the Frenchman you got paired up with then? Not too voracious, I hope? :-)

So, where did he stay, then? Sorunda, I guess… because it would be too risky to be on your own elsewhere?… wherever you might live nowadays… :-)

I almost sound like my grandma. She's always so worried. Poor thing. It can't be easy to be so worried all the time, I think!

I guess our French Class will be tighter as a group, now that you've managed hosting their visit here in Stockholm.

2002.07.10: Her father works from

Capsule Letter to myself 2

Because you had to work together as a team to make their stay as good as possible. Are you nervous about your stay in "Paris"? I can't wait! I would probably feel devastated if I were to miss that trip.

Math, Annica... keep up the fight, trying to pay off! Before you give up on one thing, try one more time! *hugs*

You know what, honey? Dave, the guy that I fancy... I haven't seen him since the end of school, even though it would be necessary... but you have done that, you little rascal :-).

I was just wondering what you came up with. Are you together, maybe? I don't think he would understand me. Hm.

But otherwise, I think he will be a wonderful friend. Oh, how complicated! The more I think about it, the more annoyed I get.

You understand my dilemma.

Are the BUP meetings helping anything? How did Dave take it? Not that it might matter ... it's for my sake that I'm going there. But I kind of wonder... my first actual meeting is next week.

2002.07.10: home daily. Mom is away

PAPER-THIN

Oh, you! You don't have any braces! *happy for you*

You did not have to have it (in the top row) on the group photo at school! Did I look good? I hate the waiting time after the photo shoot *sighs*.

I will celebrate with a lot of noise, eat a cinnamon bun, and just cuddle. I will also brush my teeth for a very long time!

I was going to give you some advice.

Hug someone every day; it benefits everyone :-).

Make sure the twins have an outstanding 18th birthday celebration; they had the fewest celebrations this year.

Be frugal with the money, but treat yourself to something once in a while; you deserve it! :-)

Film your 18th birthday, maybe for the 50th birthday present for yourself... what do I know :-).

2002.07.10: Can Mom get consolation

Capsule Letter to myself 2

Send out applications for summer jobs as soon as possible! Let's have not another wasteful summer... you feel terrible about it, but it may also depend on the circumstances *thinks*.

Try going on a trip with B1, Haiwor, and M1. You need to do something together.

Maybe you could get a summer job at the cemetery and apply early in Nynäs. Think about it anyway.

I can't think of anything else that I should tell you, except that you should enjoy the moments in life more. You may complain; it's a human right, but do it in moderation. There are people who are worse off, people who don't complain because they know others who are worse off than them. Think about that.

You little sparrow eye fly over the meadows. Dream your dreams as long as you feel alive.

Write a letter for next Christmas or so...

I think Annica will also be happy to receive a letter... from you :-).

2002.07.10: at BUP? The girl want

Then you can remind her she has to go to Cafe Birger again! I miss that time *sighs*. We often went to the cafe there for a while :-).

Merry Christmas and Happy New Year!

Can't you build a snow lantern somewhere so others can be happy when they pass by? If there is now enough snow.

:-)

Kiss and hug you, my sweetie!

Take good care of yourself and my friends.

smack /Annica

Managing the facade

The municipality took a long time to decide, causing me to feel terrified about the outcome.

I tried to protect Grandma and Grandpa, but it was at my expense. It meant spending time with my family, playing charades, and pretending everything was okay.

2002.07.10: to get help for her Mom

Capsule Letter to myself 2

Given the visit we would receive from students from France with whom we had been corresponding, I was worried about what the move would mean.

The tradition was that we would act as a host family to have an English language exchange in our free time, and then it would be our turn to travel down to them and have a French language exchange. The school solved it well by allowing several of us to be like a host group for each French person... we all slept over at a classmate's house, which was a relief for me, without it having to be a big deal.

I hadn't turned 18 yet, and under no circumstances, did I want my parents to be informed about the support I was seeking elsewhere...

The social services allowed the process to be dragged out to where nothing needed to take effect until I was about to come of age.

2002.07.12: Soc don't think that a

Capsule Letter to myself 3

To be opened at X-mas Eve 2003
Tuesday 24th of December 2002,
10.26 am

Merry Christmas and Happy New Year!

Oh, Annica, you do not know how happy I am about the letter I got from you! I have to comment on things you wrote before I give admonishments to you. Oh, you future Annica :-). First... Café Birger... *laughs* I also miss that coffee time that we had in the first grade, but I have actually been there :-) I was supposed to be there on the Trainee week... I practiced there for 1 ½ days... it's probably not so many who have done :-).

We had too many trainee students because of a mistake that was made. Therefore, I moved from Birger (now called Kòfi) to their daughter's cafe, which my supervisor's brother was running. I don't know if this experience destroyed my memories of the Birger era, but I have a new view of the Cafe.

2002.07.12: police rapport would

Capsule Letter to myself 3

They have redone, redecorated, and started a new atmosphere. And one thing is clear... they're the type of people who take advantage of trainees for cheap labor *snort*

It's been a long time since I was there having coffee and just sitting around, you know *sighs with longing*.

Something I hoped for in August was that this with BUP would lead somewhere... it has! The thing is that we could not deal with the "trauma," but they are there to help me cope with this situation so far.

I did not need Harriet after a while, so now I only go to Birgitta at BUP (and her assistants, of course).

Those in Nynäs who work at the social services ... Farzana especially ... have not done their job, and it's so annoying :-(.

Otherwise, not much has happened on that road... I still live in my cold room in this shabby village.

It's so unbelievable. My friends and I concluded it was downright sick.

2002.07.12: benefit the girl & she

PAPER-THIN

A few years ago, Denny Boy was in a relationship with Milla, and now he's with her little sister! Isn't that ridiculous?! I almost laughed myself to death when I heard that! :-) I mean, it's quite obvious that I have to get out of here!... where there are new people :-).

Something that raises hope, at least, is that they are looking for a contact family for me... well, you should probably start with that when you have done the investigation, anyway. I'm really worried... who knows what the investigation will lead to? *thinks about it* Yes! You know it, Annica! :-)

I know what I have now, but I need to move... I hardly think it would be worse, but sometimes you can wonder what it is I'm getting into *worried*.

The consequences harm not only me but everyone around me. "Harm" is perhaps a bit too drastic... it is a harsh way to put it :-)...

I would rather say that everyone is affected in some way. I hardly dare think about what grandma and grandpa would say.

2002.11.21: doesn't want them to

Capsule Letter to myself 3

By the way, Dad has just ruined my Christmas spirit! Oh, how I hate him... here I am sitting and having a great time in my solitude with you, with Christmas songs, tea, and unopened packages... then he comes and steals the Christmas music and the whole Christmas atmosphere.

On top of that, he tries to make me the villain by giving ME a bad conscience. Using sarcasm is the worst thing you can do! "Thanks for the loan then."

At least I got the music back, but how good is it, anyway? He has ruined the whole thing! *trying to gather myself to continue the letter*

I'm sorry, honey. Maybe I'm ruining your Christmas spirit. It's not my fault, but it would be stupid if you etched this feeling so that you always had it on Christmas Eve morning. Where was I?

Well,... something I didn't understand was why you were wondering how Dave took it with the BUP *ponders* Anyway, it actually took a hell of a long time before I decided what to do... and once I did, it took an eternity before I told him *bites my lip*.

2002.12.04: investigate anything

PAPER-THIN

We never got together; it didn't feel quite right... You do not know how hard it was to bring it up!... or well, future Annica, you do (if you haven't forgotten, which I hope you haven't)

Me: "How does it feel?"

Him: "You know, like when you have a bullet through your head..."

Me: "Yes..." *with pain in the facial expression*

Him: "But you also have an axe in your back..."

It was horrible! But it was good that we had managed it.

So here we are afterward. It still feels like the right thing to do. We have nothing to talk about. *Ha!* But the thing is that it's not an uncomfortable silence.

At least, I don't think so. It's almost as if he's a part of me. I know it sounds sick! Others who say that talk about falling in love, etc.

2002.12.04: Soc accepts that

Capsule Letter to myself 3

Dave has a girlfriend now, and he looks very happy... I'm happy for him, and of course, it's weird at the same time. They got together shortly after "the day."

But... yes, there is a hard truth. *sighs* Well, sweetie... You probably thought it would never happen, but we don't even talk to each other :-). But, yeah... it gets better.

I would have gotten rid of both braces for Christmas. Apparently, two teeth were crooked, and now I have to wait until January for them to remove the braces on the lower row. :-) *yippie*.

But it is true, as you say, I have no braces on the upper row, and I am so happy about it! It felt fun to get rid of them before the yearly photo shoot at school. :-) Yes, I look great!

You don't notice the row beneath :-). For some strange reason, this, with the school photos, does not feel so important anymore.

Now you will hear something fun. Under the Christmas tree was number 24 of the Christmas calendar... I got a big photo album from Bea. Thank you, thank you Bea.

2002.12.04: "Let's wait until she's 18"

PAPER-THIN

There was also the package from B1: a cup of tea, blueberry jam, a mini candy cane (that fit in the tree), and candy canes. Thank you, thank you, B1.

And in the Christmas stocking, what do you think was there? A scratch bingo ticket. What do you think happened? Annica won 100 bucks! *yippie*

M1's package will come later because it was ordered from somewhere :-). Also, we have not had the mini Christmas with our classmates, but I am looking forward to it :-).

I realized myself when I was writing Christmas cards. I was incredibly optimistic about the coming year. We will have so much fun! The 18th birthday, the France trip, the trip with B1, Haiwor, M1, and Timpa, summer jobs, maybe a move, the love maybe, we will start the third grade and be on Rudandagen.

This year, I must participate and experience Lucia! I have been sick on that day for two years now :-(.

2003.01.20: The girl is exhausted

Capsule Letter to myself 3

Honey, I hope you are happy. Thrive where you live, still have your friends, kept good contact with Sandy. Have you experienced love? I certainly hope so. It would be so wonderful to say that you are in love!

I can't think of anything that I would advise you to do.

Do you still have plans for the "Are-you-in-Collective"?

We've just found out about it :-).

I think I'll skip this with the admonitions, but I should have a New Year's resolution.

I think it will be necessary to fill Bea's photo album with experiences from 2003. Well, so be it.

Annica, have I kept that promise? :-) I wonder what the album looks like in your time.

So it works :-)

Merry Christmas and Happy New Year!

Lots of kisses / Annica

2003.01.20: & can't take any more

Dear Diary 6

Wednesday 1st of January 2003, 5.14 pm

Hi there. Here's the girl who overanalyses everything! New Year's Eve.

It's crazy how little it takes to get your life moving. Just a small response that suggests that a feeling is reciprocated can completely disrupt your entire existence. Others might call this state of being drunk... well, maybe that's true *thinking* but nothing beats that feeling in your stomach when you realize he will not reject you, but that it's actually okay.

We sat several people just above the stairs, and between me and Bea, he sat. I was unsocial as usual, but my fingers played a little with the seam of his jeans. The longer the conversation on the stairs went on, the more natural it became to caress his legs, lean against him, kiss his neck... be close to him. Letting the tip of your nose touch soft, bare skin is one of the coziest things.

Dear Diary 6

I was filled with an overwhelming sense of fear, dreading the possibility of him moving my hand, my rejection, and ultimately being completely ignored by him. I mean… you rarely get that close.

Instead, he puts his hand on my thigh and leaves it there, kissing me softly and letting me continue to cuddle while he continues to take part in the discussion.

I am indebted to Bea. She saved my evening. First, without her, I would not have been in the state I was in. Also, she asked him if I could use him as a pillow.

"Sure, do what you want," was the answer. Talk about a punch line. I probably wouldn't have even dared to lean on him without that.

People went downstairs; we were alone. There was an empty room… we met in silence. Without a word, we were tightly bound together. Close, close, close, close, close, close… and you want nothing more than to get even closer. *Draws a deep sigh*

It was a breathtaking experience. And it didn't go too far either… he respected me.

2003.01.20: suitable home & will

PAPER-THIN

But wonderful is short... Emy wanted to go home. I have now forgiven her. We are friends again (not that she ever thought we were enemies).

I must admit I couldn't help biting her shoulder when we came home to Katy again. Now we're even! * haha! *. It was probably for the best, after all.

I mean... it's true. As the TV host Arne Weise says, "It's better to stop when it's still good than to drag it out..."

The risk is that it will otherwise be a flop, you know?

I will live on this experience forever... How long will he live on it? I can't help but think about it. And what does he tell his friends? Mmm... I think I'm quite happy that we didn't exchange numbers. We didn't talk, but it was in the heat of the moment, so to speak. Relationships are based on conversations.

2003.01.20: start an internal

Dear Diary 7

Wednesday 15th of January 2003, 8.15 pm

Three photos of the last diary pages before the move

The envisioning of moving out

"This is so scary... but I do it anyway". Because there is no turning back or other options, it is probably the common denominator through my choices that led me here.

My whole body vibrates with equal parts fear and adrenaline. While the loneliness of my family echoes inexorably. Nausea rises as I describe what it was like to leave home.

PAPER-THIN

I imagine that for many young people, it is an exciting step to move out and stand on their own two feet. That's how I would have liked it to be. When I was little, my grandmother gave me a wedding chest, which she helped me fill with valuable items for the day I would be in charge of my home. Her embroidered tablecloths prepared me for the holidays, and she taught me about home economics with words like income, expenses, balance, and keeping a careful cash book. I bought the glassware I thought would suit my future home and found inexpensive towels for my wedding chest. I carved my butter knives in the wood shop, and the pine wall clock became as smooth as a baby's bottom after much sanding and polishing. This was something positive, according to my woodwork teacher.

In school, we planned fictitious floor plans for future student housing with the furniture we wanted and how we would make ends meet. I dreamed of a crystal chandelier in the bathroom, even though many people reminded me you can't have just any lighting in wet rooms. "I'll just have to find a solution to that when the time comes," I smiled back. But the move away from home did not turn out quite as I had imagined...

2003.01.20: as a shelter's in place

Moving out

The 13th of March 2003, the week before my 18th birthday. Social Services called me in the evening and told me that tomorrow was the day. They had finally confirmed a shelter for me.

After we hung up the phone, I sat on the carpet and stared ahead. My girl's room was so thoroughly cleaned, unlike the rest of our home, as I had made it a coping strategy to emphasize that you can clean up this hell, even if no one else tried in this home. But the next night, I would not sleep in this room because there was another room waiting for me at the new foster family's home.

The social workers would come with the car and pick me up so we could go to the shelter, so the bag needed to be packed.

Still empty inside from the sudden news, I went to my mother in the kitchen and said I was leaving home tomorrow. I don't remember her response or know if she believed me, but I went to my room and packed up my most important things.

2003.02.06: At school she read

PAPER-THIN

During the night, I slept poorly, if at all... Anxiety bubbled inside me, and fear swirled around how my dad would react when they arrived.

The next day, I stayed in my room with our cat on my lap, waiting for the car to arrive.

The cat's soft fur would shed, leaving black and white hairs on my sleeves, and she would reach out to pet her under the chin. This creature had been my best friend, keeping secrets I couldn't even entrust to my diary. It felt heavy to leave her now.

My cell phone rang; the social workers had turned into our street and were almost there.

I stepped out into the hall and opened our green front door. On my way to the car parked on the street, I noticed my father standing in our driveway, uncomprehending. Two young social workers with whom I had previously had contact got out of the car, and one of them followed me into the house and helped me carry my bag out.

2003.02.06: 'Alexandra's Room'.

Dear Diary 7

My blood boiled when I saw the other social worker happily socializing with Dad in the driveway as we settled into the compact car. Mom looked after us through the patio door to the kitchen, waving goodbye as we always did growing up. This time, I could only look away, and I tried my best not to break down.

The social worker in the front passenger seat exclaimed in shock when she realized it: "Oh, it was your father?!"

I held myself together, even though I swore inside that I could have torn her apart.

Not until we drove a few hundred meters did I realize I had left my Hippo stuffed animal at home on the bed, and the tears started rolling down my cheeks.

2003.03.13: Time to secretly visit

Dear Diary 8

Friday 28th of March 2003, 4.59 pm

There's a boy in my parallel class who is just so cozy …

Sure, I've liked him since the first time I talked to him… (he's one of those guys that's hard not to like…), but not in the same way as now.

I've been thinking about him constantly for about five days now.

If I sit and talk to someone, it doesn't matter what we're talking about; it doesn't matter. I squeeze him in somehow. I don't know how I do it… He's in my head; sometimes, I don't notice it because it's become so natural.

When he walks down the hallway, I want to throw myself into his arms—as if it's the most natural thing in the world. I want to hug him for ages!

Now that I feel this horrible, I'm living in chaos, with everyone running around in their thoughts…

2003.03.13: the family shelter.

Dear Diary 8

He stops, smiles at me... sees me, hears me!

He is one of the few who understands me without me having to explain a lot; at least, that's how it feels. He is there, and it feels so incredibly nice.

Does this mean I'm in love? It feels so weird... I've forgotten what it was like... even repressed it, to avoid being hurt.

I complicate everything... it's me who makes everything so difficult... I think so much, worry, and keep going.

I don't want to hurt him!

I'm so afraid that I'll play with his feelings... it sounds stupid, I know... but I don't want to ruin his relationship with his girlfriend for some feeling that I'm not even sure I have.

God, how tired I get of myself! I want to live, enjoy all the moments, and not have to worry about the consequences beforehand.

2003.03.14: The next day she moved.

PAPER-THIN

I'm lying on a couch, hearing his breathing... closing my eyes... hearing the guy's joking comments about the mistakes made at the pool table, laughing...

Before my birthday, a bunch of us had an internal discussion about dates on birthdays... the discussion returned because of "some people's" poor memory :-). Anyway, I was thrilled that he remembered... it has its explanation, it turned out... he showed up at my surprise party! Seeing him there made my evening. Without him, it wouldn't have been the same at all. But of course... a few days later, I was worried about whether I had messed up. I know that, in retrospect, I asked if I had been difficult... he didn't understand what I was referring to, and I didn't dare clarify myself.

I have the feeling that I was quite pushy... I probably crossed the line. Not that anything happened, but if you assume he has a girlfriend, then ... no, I wouldn't have been so happy if I had been his girlfriend, Jonna and knew about it.

2003.03.14: & remained for 100 days

Dear Diary 8

At the dinner at Bea's house during the sports holiday... we ate tacos and went for a walk in the middle of the night... that day, the social secretary from Nynäs was supposed to call. She never called, and everything felt so hopeless... I've been through this before. They don't do their job as they should.

I felt so small and sad in my helplessness. That night, he held my hand ... all night. It meant so much. Thinker Annica came into the picture. I don't like her; she always over-analyses things.

Anyway, it was super cozy... there is no other way to describe it.

I think I tried to blame myself for the tingling in my stomach as if it were forbidden while the rest of the room remained unaware.

Dave is going to Spain, and I won't see him for a week. I wonder how Jonna feels. Is it the same thing?

It would have been nice to see him before he leaves, but this gives me time to think things through... advantage/disadvantage?

Sigh

2003.06.04: She was no longer single

PAPER-THIN

What's the time? Seems it's already morning.

I see the sky, it's so beautiful and blue.

The TV's on, but the only thing showing a picture of you.

Oh, I get up and make myself some coffee.

I try to read a bit, but the story's too thin.

I thank the Lord above you're not here to see me in this shape I'm in.

Spending my time, watching the days go by

Feeling so small, I stare at the wall.

Hoping that you think of me too.

I'm spending my time

Annica, singing like the band Roxette

2003.06.23: Girls' shelter opened

Capsule Letter to myself 4

To be opened on 9th of July 2004
Saturday 12th of June 2004, 10.19 pm

Dear Annica!

I have sat down with pen and paper in the middle of waiting for the election results and the match between Spain and Russia to write a letter to you, Annica. Yes, and it's not just that, by the way... I have a good reason for sitting here.

On Monday, I start a summer job, for the second year in a row, at Ericsson in Nynäshamn. I'm not exactly looking forward to it, but it will go quickly... four weeks :-). With this letter, you, Annica, can reflect on your time at Ericsson and think about how it turned out... it wasn't so bad. :-) My mom works during all my weeks, and I think that's good.... I'll probably eat with them this year, too,... right?

I will miss Dave... but it can be helpful!

My attitude... well, I'll try to cheer myself up...

2004: Even though she lived there

PAPER-THIN

Clever motto note on the door

Tidy room

Clothes that feel just right and mascara!

A cheerful mood (that's how you treat people!)

Breakfast every morning!!!

In addition, with the help of a cross almanac and birth control pills, I will keep track of the countdown :-) The boss is not so dangerous... it's just his strange humor that makes it *hm* You do not have to hang out anyway :-)

Well... there was another thing I was thinking about, too...

Tomorrow, I will probably find out if the sign language and deaf-blind interpreter program at Södertörns Folkhögskola (Secondary) School in Haninge has admitted me. You have indeed received an answer, Annica... and you have made a choice, too. What did you choose? How did it go?

2004: she preferred being at her boyfriend's

Capsule Letter to myself 4

I am still trying to figure out what to do if I get into both places... Umeå is nice, but so far away... four years in Haninge is perhaps a little too close.

Do the plus and minus lists work?

You, dear me, in four weeks, I hope you followed your heart's voice. That's what Dave told you to do. "Everything will work out."

Forget him! That would be the biggest mistake of your life! He is my everything, my treasure, my heart's friend, the apple of my eye, my foil, and my security. His hand is in mine, and I follow him. Of course, I should not let my opportunities be diminished just because he wants to live his life. I will encourage and support him in all his choices, just as he will be there for me when I have to make mine.

Kisses to you, girl... and take care!

Annica

P.S "Don't forget that you are valuable."

2004: and soon she practically lived there.

Annica, I want to wish you and your feet ALL THE BEST!

How wonderful it is to be finally free of warts.

Take good care of yourselves and never allow them to come back.

Every day: Wash and lubricate.

1 day/week: Take a foot bath, peel, file, and lubricate. Take care of your nails, too.

Many warm hugs! D.S

I just wanted to live a normal life

It's unclear in my writing, but yes, Dave and I eventually got together. He came home from Spain, and I spent an entire afternoon sitting in the phone booth in the empty school building, getting the courage to call him and tell him how I felt.

The cleaner came by and just laughed at me. "Boy, trouble," he giggled and went on. He just understood.

Capsule Letter to myself 4

At the end of my second year of high school, there was a party at the home of one of my classmates. Since then, we have been inseparable, except he had to break up with his girlfriend first.

I can't say how much it meant to me, how he and his family welcomed me with open arms.

I lived in the shelter for 100 days and made the comparison that if the contestants in the reality show Big Brother made it, so did I, just like them.

Even though the foster family did their best, I felt uncomfortable. The adult son had an intellectual disability and was happy to help fold my underwear after the laundry had dried. I caught his sister, who also still lived at home, masturbating on the living room couch several times.

This time was manageable because another girl also moved in shortly after me. It was nice to chat with someone who was in a similar situation and understood me.

What happened to her afterward? I wonder.

2004: she wanted a "normal" family.

PAPER-THIN

The municipality informed me they were setting up a girls' shelter with staff on-site during the day to provide us with continuous support. I was welcome to move there from the shelter.

It was a big two-story apartment with an enormous hall, toilet, living room, kitchen, and staff office on the ground floor. And upstairs there were three bedrooms, a bathroom, toilet, a small TV room and another entrance.

As this was a new start-up, it echoed empty when I was also moving in myself.

In retrospect, something that was unclear was how the relationship with my family continued.

I know that through Child and Youth Psychiatry, I encouraged my mother to get counseling support, and I worked with her at Ericsson during the summer and enjoyed it.

The relationship with my father also led to some reconciliation, and none of this was explicitly mentioned to Dave's parents. I never told them what I was subjected to as a child, and a kind of facade was once again kept up….

2004: Her parents joined for dinner

Capsule Letter to myself 4

My grandmother and grandfather were also important in my life; even in my relationship with them, I had to play charades.

I chose not to contact other relatives, family, and friends. This is not because it wouldn't have been fun to have these relationships, but to make it easier for myself and not have to wear the mask that everything is as it should be.

I got into the sign language and deaf-blind interpreter program in the same building as my high school. It was nice that it didn't mean another move for that reason, but I eventually got a 1st hand contract within walking distance to the school (although I still mostly hung out at Dave and his family's house).

2004.12.15: No longer in need of BUP

Capsule Letter to myself 5

To be opened at NewYear's 2007
Sunday 31st of December 2006, 1 pm

Hello, my dear Annica! Happy New Year!

It has been a long time since I wrote to myself... and my previous letters have somehow disappeared with my moves. I, therefore, cannot respond to "then-time Annica's" musings. But what does it matter? It's a new time now. It's time to send it forward.

But first, I thought I'd reflect on the past year, 2006 :-).

Tomorrow marks one year since I was at John and Helena's house for the first time. It's pretty cool because, during the year, I've gotten to know them much better. I met my passion—climbing! Oh, how wonderful it has been—26 meters!

It's something that I don't want to lose.

I got rid of my verrucas! I only have one last check-up left. I will book it soon. It is so wonderful!

2004.06.04: She graduated and soon

Capsule Letter to myself 5

My first treatment was on the 5th of January 2006. Oh, how I have struggled, so I sit here a year later wart free :-) Nice!

The school? Yes, I have to divide it into the spring semester and the fall semester.

Spring semester: It was hard, it was. But there were quite delightful pieces, too. We were active in the deaf church and the sign choir. It was both fun and exciting, and the congregation appreciated it. Too bad it had to be closed down :-(.

All these presentations were very heavy, but they were well-planned. The guided tour at the Nordic Museum where I got to talk about the exhibition "Norwegians and Swedes," the Malmö presentation with Mio... or my presentation about Hjalmar Söderberg where Anders pinched my manuscripted notes just before I was about to start... AND I DID IT! What a feeling :-).

Then came the exam week... 2/5 - 5/5 2006 v.18

2005.02.01: she had a new apartment

PAPER-THIN

It never feels good with exams, and this exam week was not so different from others. Afterward, it felt like that… but I wasn't particularly worried. What was so annoying was that… I didn't see it coming. The evaluation of the test came as a shock to me.

What is so disturbing about Södertörn is that everything is so unspoken. It wasn't like they brought up and talked about what had happened. After you had evaluated individually, you could have had the discussion with the entire class. It was so strange to go on summer vacation… the entire atmosphere was so scary. For this reason, this year's price goes to… *drumroll*… Södertörns Folkhögskola (Secondary) School!

Another reason is that the school placed the test the week after the last day of application to the university and other programs. Everyone knows the deadline is April 15. The school, if anyone, should know it!

In retrospect, I'm glad I received the message that I'm not ready to interpret (But I object to how someone delivered the message and its circumstances!) Otherwise, I would have continued on the same path without reflecting.

2005: The education to become an

Capsule Letter to myself 5

There is probably a meaning to everything.

During the summer, I took 18 lessons at the traffic school. Unfortunately, I still have no driver's license and no motivation. Dave and I were at Play in the concert hall. We went to Gothenburg with John, Helena, and the children. It was very fun :-) Then we spent a lot of time in the cottage. I did not work this year either, so now it stings a little in the wallet. I am motivated to work, you can't even imagine.

Incidentally, it was this year that Robin was in Big Brother. Disturbed... but fun! :-) Even today, you can read about him in the Evening paper, but thankfully not through what he has done but through the winning Jessica, his girlfriend.

Fall semester: Living at Västanviks Folkhögskola (Secondary) School has been instructive. I have gotten to know myself and nice people.

2006: interpreter was too hard, but

PAPER-THIN

I now know that I don't want to be an interpreter and that I belong in Stockholm. I have found my creative spirit. Crafts have been on the shelf for a while, but I have gotten to feel how important it is for me to craft. Marie has been inspiring me at so many levels, and for that, I'm truly grateful :-).

I started exercising differently and got to try Pilates. Fun!

I have benefited from my gym card.

I read "Self-esteem Now!" by Mia Törnblom, and it has impressed me. Without it, I probably would not have had the courage to move home to Stockholm.

I have managed without TV, well... yes, of course. I had a TV, but I didn't use it very often.

The only programs I followed I saw in the TV room with others who were as stuck as me :-) "Desperate Housewives," "Ugly Betty," "Lasse-Maja's Detective Agency."

Capsule Letter to myself 5

As it looks today, my home address is back to being registered in Sorunda. (I have to sign the papers and send them in), but I hope it's short term!

Dear future Annica!

I hope you are in good health, that you've continued climbing, and that you've found a place/form of exercise that suits you. I also hope you enjoy it and feel good when you perform.

I hope you are eating a healthy, wholesome diet. Because that is something that goes hand in hand with health and exercise :-).

What does your life look like? It's exciting because I have no idea :-).

Where do you work? Where do you live? Do you thrive? I want you to do that... thrive, that is. The most important thing is still to listen to the heart's voice.

New Year's resolution? Well...

I want to drink less alcohol ... or ... reduce my alcohol intake, you might say.

2006: her passion of expression.

PAPER-THIN

I want to be more environmentally conscious.

I want to find a job that suits me.

I want to find a home for Dave and me where we both feel comfortable.

I want to continue exercising.

I want to find myself… or get to know myself even better :-).

I wish you all the happiness and that you live in harmony with yourself!

"I am the most important in my life."

I love you! Kisses and hugs!

Annica

2006: As the year ended, she took

Dear Diary 9

Wednesday 16th of April 2008

Dear Diary, these are the notes from the Session at Blue Lotus when I met the clairvoyant medium.

ARCHANGELS:

Michael - Protects with his sword.

Rafael - Helps with healing.

Gabriel - Supports communication and creativity (writing!)

Maria - The courageous warmth. I have a lot of energy.

ENDURANCE: When I set my mind to something, I am very goal-oriented and patient as long as I decide.

2007: a leap & followed her heart.

PAPER-THIN

SELF-DETERMINATION: Taking on a pre-formed job within a professional framework can be tricky. I need more than being a student assistant to live a full life. Running my business could be something.

TREATMENT: In a group that I like, I spread harmony. I am an asset with my insights and ideas... and my sensitivity.

SPEAKER: I can reach out to a larger group of people... today I find it difficult to understand, but it is undoubtedly essential knowledge for the future.

BRIDGE BUILDER: I will psychologically understand people, sense groups, and moods, and through that, be able to act as a bridge builder, a link.

STRUCTURE: For me, it is super important! Order, accuracy, clarity.

2007: That lead to her dream job.

Dear Diary 9

VISION: In my life, people come and go. Everyone contributes to my achieving my vision. Be grateful for all the contributions/exchanges. I will take in what I need and stay true to the vision. When people and things leave, it is important to have clear endings, as no unresolved conflicts should remain. I will reach my dreams, but I must work hard for them.

NOW: It has been a difficult period, but I am coming out of it. I am in a spiritual phase. I have come a long way and seen something unlimited beyond this world. But there is more to discover, see more clearly, etc.

I connect with this spirituality when I create, write, and meditate.

WRITE: Writing is not an achievement. It is just for me. I write journals and poems, and I keep a book close at hand during meditation to record the words that come to me.

MEDITATION: This can involve being in nature, contemplating, feeling calm, and being careful not to overexert myself in everyday life.

2008: Using sign language to

PAPER-THIN

FUTURE: It is about different meetings. Exchanges between people... relationships from previous lives, etc. It is about resolving attachments and old conflicts. To move forward and closer to the vision, you need to walk upright without carrying a lot of unresolved issues.

NUTRITION: You can treat yourself sometimes, but it's still essential to think about what you're putting into your body. There is something nice about giving yourself the best of the best in terms of health.

LOVE: It is radiant. There are many beautiful things ahead of me. Family life, children... It will do me good. In relationships, I must stand my ground and take my place. "I AM HERE. I NEED THIS"

It takes an inner strength and a realization that I am worth it. If I respect myself, so do others.

PROFESSION: Being a student assistant is not enough. Creation is a common thread throughout my life.

2008: support pupils with

BARRIERS: I will come across blockages... then "just" put them aside, look at them, and move on. Take the battles and STAND UP FOR YOURSELF. I am the right one.

CONTRACTS: "Read contracts carefully, even the fine print, when signing anything." This is important to not get ripped off.

PROJECTS: I have many strings on my bow, so there is a lot going on at once. It's important for me to think, "Okay, now I'm done," when I finish a project.

Staying in the old makes me stagnant (and inhibits creativity?).

HARNESS CREATIVITY... I HAVE MORE THAN MOST PEOPLE.

2008: disabilities was such a joy.

Dear Diary 10

Wednesday 11th of March 2009, 07.15 am

It's itchy, and I don't know what to do.

Call the youth clinic and make an appointment. How many times will I have to do that? How many times do I have to put effort into all the treatments? *thinking about what I have written*.

Oh I realised I was in victim mode...

I have to put in that time and effort if I want to get rid of my itchy genitals.

No one else is going to do it for me. It's my responsibility to take care of myself!

The last time I was there, the doctor had a hypothesis that it could be the hormone in the contraceptive that was causing it, but not since I have been without contraception for some time now.

2009: A colleague introduced her to

Dear Diary 11

Saturday 14th of March 2009, 11.55 am

When I was younger and still living at home in Sorunda, I was a perfectionist at cleaning every Thursday. It was dusting, wiping everything on the shelf... all the skincare products... all the books... making sure all the papers were where they should be, symmetrically and carefully.

Vacuuming and wet wiping were a must.

Change of bedding, shaking off/weathering of pillows and duvet. Depending on the season and weather, I felt the urge to even shake or whip the carpets.

All surfaces needed to be wiped, preferably also where they were difficult to reach, such as behind the bed and at the back of the cupboard.

I talked to the flowers for the sake of the oxygen. All this was to show that the rest of the house's clutter was not okay. In order to express the aggression and hatred that I felt.

2009: Debbie Ford's Shadow Process.

PAPER-THIN

To create, for my sake, an environment that I felt I could stay in. To clarify, it was possible to maintain order… that it was possible to have a pleasant environment at home, to invite people over without feeling ashamed.

2009: A retreat in Copenhagen and

Dear Diary 12

Saturday 14th of March 2009, 1.50 pm

It is with trembling fingers I write this. I don't know what I want to get out of reading this letter.

I want to forgive and put this behind that strengthens me for who I am today. Do I want to answer the letter? I do not know. Yes, I want to, but I don't know if it's being sent.

It's for my sake to let go.

It is completely idiotic to have a box you are afraid of that follows you year after year. You are terrified of opening it. It should be there. Over the years, it has been important to me. It has been there, hidden away with the lid on. When I've accused others of ignoring it, of putting the lid on, it's actually me who has done it.

It's so clear to me now. Once I opened the little box, I was afraid to touch the crumpled paper.

PAPER-THIN

I feel a little scared, shaky, alone, responsible for a family together, furious. I know it's not true, but that's still my feeling.

I forgive myself for taking all the blame. It's time to read the letter after all these years...

I have now read the letter and responded to it, crying, sniveling, and sobbing my way through it. As Debbie Ford says, "Breathe into that feeling."

Six A4 pages, and I feel much lighter. I still haven't read through what I wrote and haven't decided what I want to do with it, but it's nice to have it out and down on paper.

The funny thing is when I started thinking about how long ago it was; I realized that today is exactly six years since I left home. Six years to the day. On 14th of March 2003, I left home, with the help of the Social Services, to the foster family in Trollbäcken.

Did I write this today?

Strange

It has already become night.

2009: shadow work, helped her dwell

Dear Diary 12

Today has been an excellent day for me. I really took the time to write forgiveness lists and letters. I spent the entire afternoon doing this, and it was so lovely. In my wildest imagination, I would not have thought I would open my shrine if someone had asked me a month ago.

It's a massive thing for me. Understand that it has been weighing on me for six years. Unbelievable!

That I then looked through my scrapbook "junk" in the shoebox and could clear out a whole pile felt great! There are certainly many areas that would be nice to clean out.

Dear Diary 13

Saturday 13th of June 2009, 11.40 am.

Last night, my mom gave me Reiki. It was very pleasant and calmed me down. I combined it with a visit to my Internal Garden.

I tried their new shower this morning, and it felt wonderfully fresh. I then sat down and read the letters I wrote to my parents and then what I wrote in my diary, all of which encouraged me to reach my 90-day goal. With my support in mind, I feel calm.

"There is nothing to be afraid of."

"I am safe, no matter what."

"I need this work with myself."

9:15 pm

I HAVE GIVEN THE LETTERS TO MY PARENTS!!!

I sat down on their couch and mentioned that I thought I was ready to talk about leaving home.

Dear Diary 13

There was silence at first. But after picking for a while, they both sat down... and even though it was a tense atmosphere, it was still relaxed.

Being able to refer my thoughts to my grandmother's beach ball made me feel safe.

We then discussed child education and their goals and views on it as parents of young children.

My father told me that his goal from the beginning was to be strict at first so that he could relax over time, which gave me a new perspective.

He was happy and satisfied that we had become as decent as we are today. But he was jealous of my grandfather, who could be the playful father. It's hard to know what's right from the start. He had some regrets.

I said he would have to make up for it as a grandfather later. It comes naturally, then.

2009: with herself and her parents.

I can't quite believe I've handed over the letters. I thanked them for accepting them, and for me, the important thing is not to get an answer but that I have handed them over. It is symbolic that I have given up what I have been carrying. I will probably only understand when they have read the letters.

"Hey, I made it. I'm the world's greatest …"

I thought I knew what forgiveness looked like

I feel like there is so much anger in my journals and I have sent none of the letters I wrote to my family, except those two mentioned in my diary on Saturday, 13th of June 2009.

My mom and dad were handed one letter each, and I feel like they needed to be here to balance my story and help me understand my timeline and the complete picture.

I asked my mom if she still had her letter and if I could include it in the book, but unfortunately, she couldn't find it.

2009: She fulfilled her dreams by

Dear Diary 13

The period when I wrote reconciliation letters is a missing piece of the puzzle for me. I'm not entirely sure what made me reconcile with my father after I left home, but it is the coaching course I studied at a distance. Teaching was in groups over the phone, and I was the only Swede. I also traveled to Copenhagen, Denmark, to take part in a Shadow Process Workshop with European peers.

"Forgiveness" became a big part of what I took away from my coaching, and I needed it to keep grandma and grandpa, from my father's side, in my life. That's how it felt.

In retrospect, I would have needed support and the explanation that you can "forgive" without "staying."

In the following years, I lived with a rigid and polite standard, as if nothing had happened, even though everything remained hidden under the surface.

My boyfriend invited my family to his house, and even my grandparents were there. Once again, I stepped into keeping up some kind of facade, even though that was not my original intention.

2009: studying fashion and design.

Poems written at ATSUB

At Atsub, I started writing poems. It was my boyfriend's mother who finally alerted me to the fact that things were probably not right at home with my family and helped to put me in touch with Atsub, the Association of Sexually Exploited Children.

I contacted those who worked in the association, and I even got support to connect with my mother. And I'm grateful for the healing process that unfolded through my connections at ATSUB.

I used to visit them weekly, and for some periods of my healing process, even daily, when I went through the hassle of going through the court application of the legal process, I decided to start.

One of the consistent pillars was the Writing Sessions on Thursdays that I attended together with others in similar situations. The poems were a playful way to marinate and cope with things that bothered us or would lift us up during rough times.

2009: She even created her own

Poems written at ATSUB

And as a bonus, we were offered to submit our texts that we would like to share in the annual printed book of ATSUB...

I'll share nine of them here with you as well on the upcoming pages.

Poem 1
My Values = Who Am I?
Thursday 22nd of October 2009, 12.05 am

Stylish, everything has its place, structured.

The dream of clearing out

Cleaning day, significant cleaning once a month

An apartment, without a large storage room

Whole clean garments. Essential wardrobe (preferably made by yourself)

IKEA wardrobe (My dream!)

Sprout cultivation, planting kitchen spices?

Bake your bread and buns.

2009: mannequin during a workshop.

PAPER-THIN

Keep the kitchen clean.

Holiday curtains

Authenticity

When someone makes something, they start from scratch. Craftsmanship and authenticity.

Love in every moment.

It doesn't feel right to leave something half-finished/half-decent.

Everyone should have the time to get to know themselves.

To meditate, write, and reflect is essential for me.

To create, craft, be creative, and resourceful.

To be close to nature, its changes, its life.

A good meal in the company of friends. A glass of wine, candles lit.

Curling up on the sofa with a cup of tea and down slippers.

2009: Her boyfriend that she had

Poems written at ATSUB

Knitting is my life.

My basic idea is ecological. No one can do everything, but everyone can do something. And I want to do what I can for Mother Earth.

Charity

Thoughtfulness and thought before action.

Cultural phenomena/events nourish the soul.

My bookshelf reflects me. What genre do I read?

How are the books placed/sorted?

I find it very interesting to look at other people's bookshelves.

Writes in Braille I am creative and choose an inspiring future.

2009: been living with for a while,

Poem 2
I am me, but who am I?
Tuesday 2nd of November 2010

Taking the pen feels like my first stumbling step towards an unwritten future. Surrendering without a safety net and keeping your cool is both scary and outstanding.

I am a girl who usually depends on my Tipp-Ex. To correct, rectify, and maintain a pleasant facade...

Everything should be as perfect as possible. Preferably hide what does not live up to the standard. My Tipp-Ex is my security in my writing, and it gives me an opportunity to let myself go... because I know I can always change or take back everything I have written, thanks to my Tipp-Ex.

Therefore, I have chosen not to use my white lifeline in this writing. I want to be honest with myself and, therefore, hide my Tipp-Ex for a while.

2010: started school elsewhere.

Poems written at ATSUB

Already, I can feel myself weighing every word, sentence, and phrase before I write them down. Thank goodness I haven't had a terrible spelling mistake yet... usually when that happens, I reach for my white rescue with its mushroom-covered top. Yes, because I don't think it can be just any Tipp-Ex.

An ideal Tipp-Ex, in Annica's taste, has a sponge tip, not a brush that will lose bristles and accuracy. It should definitely not be water-based—it's way too soft. The jar should contain a metal ball that shakes the Tipp-Ex properly when you shake it.

Last but not least, it should be quick-drying. Very important.

The absolute worst kind is the one that resembles a VHS tape with Tipp-Ex attached to the strip. When you pull against the paper, the strip transfers the Tipp-Ex onto the paper. On the day when this process no longer works and the strip slips out, the whole thing becomes gibberish.

2010: At the same time his mom had

Despite much talk about erasing, I still love writing. Playing with words and phrases has long captivated me. I like to add descriptive words that can change the complete text. But it's been a long time since I wrote that kind of text.

So it's great to feel the desire to write again. And it's with an exhilarating feeling that I set out without a safety net.

In good company, I have grabbed my pen.

Poem 3
If an observer were to describe me.
Thursday 4th of November 2010

"Good girl," she said sweetly, patting my nose with her index finger. My colleague, who is approaching retirement. In the next breath, behind my back, she said, "But she is so young."

She is a quiet and thoughtful girl with no answers… but once she opens her mouth, she stuns everyone with her wisdom.

A domesticated girl who likes routines, order, writing lists, planning, and structuring.

Poems written at ATSUB

A liberated girl who loves to jump in piles of leaves in the fall, kick the leaves, and listen to the rustling around her shoes.

A cinnamon bun lover! Cinnamon Bun Day is her holiday, and she celebrates it with all bells and whistles. It is a day where she stays in people's memories.

Loving and caring. Caring, crafty, and creative. Creative.

Wonderful to be around. Calmness spreads. It's fun to spend time with her happy, playful side.

A cultural girl who likes to come up with new crazy antics. Sightseeing events that no one has ever heard of. Free events that feed the soul.

A misunderstood environmentalist who has lost her fire.

A strong girl who had to carry too heavy a burden on her own. A cold girl who learned to build barriers.

A hot girl who repressed moved on, and once again "put the lid on."

2010: was off. So she offered help.

(Has it ever been lifted?)

She is small inside yet strong enough / Brave enough to follow her heart's voice.

She is a beautiful person, worthy of realizing her dreams.

Poem 4
I take responsibility for myself.
Thursday 27th of January 2011

I take responsibility for my well-being and happiness. What I fill my life with is entirely up to me. What approaches and measurements should I choose?

"I am creative, and I choose an inspiring future."

"2011 is the Year of Opportunity!"

"I'm making the greatest shift of my life."

2010.10.27: First visit at ATSUB

Poems written at ATSUB

The years go by. I realize as I flip through my diary. To my dismay, I also realize how numb I have been. The same dreams, year in and year out. I find a pile of unfinished projects. I should have taken those intentions more seriously. Behavioral patterns that I used to need but which today are a burden to me. Perhaps the Ego's unwillingness to change has been my security. My dreams were a part of me, a false security, in the fear of being disappointed... if they didn't turn out exactly as I had planned.

My dreams are still a part of me... the part that now listens to my passion for life. I feel excited at the thought that I can realize them!

Poem 5
A memory
Thursday 10th of February 2011

My high school days feel distant and vague.

A strange stage in life that has long since been a closed chapter.

The everyday life of that time is barely a memory when you have deliberately hidden and forgotten to move on.

2011: Finally she met young adults

I remember little ... but I remember you ... my hugging buddy.

That was the label I gave you because no other word explains the feeling better.

Two friends meet at recess to hug. Long and without expectations.

I don't remember the first or the last hug, just the feeling of being embraced with warmth when you need it most.

Poem 6
Little One
Monday 4th of April 2011

I long for you.

To hold you and smell you.

To lose myself in your face.

Wonder like you and the wonder of the world.

I want to decorate the earth for your arrival.

Adorn it with trust and love.

2011: like herself, survivors from

Poems written at ATSUB

Cherish the land that will one day be yours.

It is you I live for. My purpose is to grow with you.

I can feel it even though you are not yet born.

I long for you, Little One.

Poem 7
Damn You!
Monday 20th of June 2011, 5.30 pm

Do you realize that you have turned my entire worldview upside down? I don't want to go back to passing you in the hallway. I need a discharge.

Shake me up. Please give me something to talk about.

My legs are bouncing, and my stomach tingles with the resulting tension.

I can't handle it!

2011: sexual abuse as children.

My view of myself and my well-being in my workplace is completely reversed. Thanks to you.

Only this, I don't have to hide at all...

I can stretch out in all my glory. Do you realize that you have helped me with that?

But now I stand here with all this insight, with no idea what to do. I thought I knew my next steps, and then you swept the rug out from under me.

Poem 8
Shadow Work: The story of my life.
Saturday 2nd of July 2011

I was born and raised in a family where love was something you earned.

Dad: a pedantic, workaholic, hypersensitive to sound. The attention I received came in screams and harsh words.

I didn't feel loved and didn't want to be loved. He has blown his cards.

Poems written at ATSUB

I feel let down and betrayed.

He is skeptical, wimpy, weird, odd, xenophobic, cautious, victim, rigid, degrading, clumsy, helpless, desperate, liar, and I get so fucking annoyed and provoked by him. (My attitude is there in the conversation. What quality/sub-personality is this?)

Mom is a loving and creative theater person. She is also down-to-earth, spiritual, and attentive to detail. I have always been able to turn to her because we share a love of life and a humorous approach to adversity and everyday life. She is tidy, just like me.

Although she has essential matters, I still feel betrayed and neglected. She didn't take my side, and it still hurt me. She's self-absorbed, chatty, uninterested... something that takes over when we speak on the phone. I become absent and uninterested.

Johan: a non-existent relationship. It's completely gone down the drain and we don't know each other at all. And it's my fault. I never explained what was going on. I just moved away. He is innocent, unprotected... I feel resigned, sad *broken heart* stiff, polite, etc.

PAPER-THIN

Shelter/Social Services: I moved to the foster home and family shelter in Trollbäcken. This was with the help of the idiot Farzana, the social secretary. She did not take her responsibility. She did not protect me as she should. Greeted my father nicely, did not understand my situation.

She is stupid, out of touch, frivolous, unprofessional, stupid, incompetent, and unsympathetic.

I feel let down and betrayed, abandoned.

Thinking about her makes me hateful, angry, and sad.

Foster Home: I lived in Trollbäcken for 100 days. A secret that I don't talk to anyone about.

I feel ashamed about this. I don't have a well-functioning family, and it was so bad that I had to decide to leave.

I want to hide this part of my story the most. I am ashamed that I had to run, hide, and put up those barriers.

2011: By trusting the process and

Poems written at ATSUB

Bryan Adams was my friend then. I started seeing Dave; we got together. I collected newspaper clippings and comments to fill my album. Kathy made it a little easier to live there... someone who understood anyway.

The abuse is a story in itself...

I feel dirty and disgusting. My entire relationship with my body is based on this, and this also affected my sexuality.

I feel sad because someone has taken something away from me. He made me sleep without panties. My mom couldn't stand the nagging and agreed with him. I feel betrayed and abandoned.

What would have been better?

A loving upbringing, close relationships, NO ABUSE! My parents would have had a loving relationship with passionate sex, so I wouldn't have been involved. *tears*

Johan and I would be tight. Strong sibling love. No facade / Keeping up appearances, no secrets.

2011: leaning on her new support,

PAPER-THIN

Imagine having a happy family with whom I would love to go on vacation. Security and being able to relax in their company. I was always on edge. I am holding up my shield and defense wall, angry.

Imagine if I would have loved to bring friends home.

(Our cat was my salvation in everything)

I have failed at Herbalife, interpreter's training, tailoring training, maintaining a healthy lifestyle, sexually, and meeting people.

I have lost my grandmother, my contact with Johan, my friends, my courage and playfulness, my money, my mobility, and my control.

I have experienced disappointment so many times... I give myself hope and then fall flat on my face. Flying at Universeum, for example. Naïve. Trusting people who do not keep what they say. Mom especially.

I regret the investment in Herbalife.

2011: she started putting up new

Poems written at ATSUB

I hope, crave, and dream of harmony, traveling, seeing the world, standing up for myself, self-esteem, speaking fluent English, passion, play, desire, health, crafts, creativity, happiness, beautiful surroundings, writing, expressing myself fully, dancing, performing, being proud to be me, a job I love to go to, freedom, financial independence, time to do everything I love, joy, beautiful, family, children and being radiant. To be genuine and authentic.

It feels like this needs to be more attainable. Even if I could get there, I would only, once again, disappoint myself. Going after the dream destroys the magic of it... by realizing them, they disappear.

The particular theme, the underlying pattern

Deceived, betrayed, unloved, abandoned, exploited, shield, protective wall, self-sabotage

Me: annoyed, resigned, hateful, angry, sad, ashamed, dirty, disgusting, naïve.

What conclusions have I made, and what are they?

What did I make that mean about me?

2011: healthy boundaries.

PAPER-THIN

I'm not good enough: 7

I am unlovable: 3

I am undeserving: 4

I can't trust anyone: 8

I am bad: 1

I'm on important: 2

Something is wrong with me: 2

I am a failure: 2

No one cares about me: 2

I don't matter: 2

I'm too stupid: 2

Conclusion: TOP 3 Shadow Believes

I can't trust anyone.

I'm not good enough

2011.10.12: She dialed her father

Poems written at ATSUB

I'm undeserving

Poem 9
Kick-Off!
Monday 26th of September 2011

I can't find any words; I'm overwhelmed by reading MY REVIEW and pages 7-14 in Alexandra's room.

Shit, shit, shit... SO enormous!

The 26th of September is a day to be celebrated and sanctified.

Something that strikes me is Alexandra's detailed descriptions. And how well Alexandra writes the book from the child's perspective.

The princess is playing and resorting to face painting for protection.

The grief over the broken mast of their bark boat.

The old grandmother tells us it is never the child's fault if the adults are stupid.

2011: to confront him & got his

PAPER-THIN

Fascinated by how safe I am to begin this process.

AND I AM SO EXCITED!

Mondays are now a favorite day.

Shit, they will mean a lot to me, and I will tell you about the triggers that might show up!

2011: confession on tape.

What-If-Letter to Dad

Thursday 13th of October 2011

Dad,

Now it's time for you to take your responsibility.

It's time you take responsibility for what you've done to me.

It's not my job to tell my little brother. I'm not the one to run your errands or solve what has been hushed up for so long.

My relationship with my little brother is the way it is today because of you, and you owe it to me to fix it.

Never again do I want to keep up your facade.

Never again will I wear the mask of politeness in front of friends and acquaintances.

It hurts and itches and leaves nasty, invisible scars.

Triggers reading

Alexandra's Room' I:
Friday 14th of October 2011

It has been almost two weeks since I last read Alexandra's room. Now, I am struck by how she described the silence.

The feeling: "We don't talk about that."

When her father is mentioned, it is her mother who shows this.

The feeling has been with me for as long as I can remember. Acceptance. I accepted this approach and could not tell my friends.

Silence is the perpetrator's best weapon, coupled with the shame of breaking it.

I remain silent because I don't know who knows what. And the silence is unbearable. Everyone plays along, nervous about what would happen otherwise.

Or is it perhaps indifference... or relief?

2011: to start coaching clients.

Triggers reading

"That doesn't concern me."

A single flat and uninspiring soup, tasteless and watery.

But everyone keeps a friendly face and eats, anyway.

2011: But it was now clear that she

Triggers reading

'Alexandra's Room' II:
Monday 17th of October 2011

That voice. I can immediately tell who you are talking to. You are talking to a child or a woman. Your voice is pretending, and you are pretending.

A child or a woman can never be equal to a man.

Politeness, politeness, degrading politeness.

The phone is handed over to a man, and there goes the facade. You can talk normally again, person to person.

It doesn't matter how old the child is... or is it because the teenager is a girl?

Someone steps in and gets too close, not respecting the zone that is my personal sphere.

And when is it okay to say no when the adults insist I must allow?

2011: instead needed therapeutic

Triggers reading

The unwritten rule is that we don't play in my house. I always want to come home to you, getaway. I'd rather be in your empty house, alone with your flowers for a whole week, then at home with my anxiety and my family.

2011: support of her own to deal

Triggers reading

"Alexandra's Room' III:
Monday 7th of November 2011

Ivan's disguised voice. That degraded voice that Dad uses to clarify who is a child/woman or an adult/man.

How Dad made me give up partying at the flatbed truck to celebrate my graduation with my family right away.

Going to his house and cleaning instead of having dinner with Dave's parents.

The feeling associated with the tree bark boat in that story: Let's do this because it's best. I'm doing it for you...

We have gathered here for your sake. We are making room to receive your moving boxes.

Mike asked me if my parents ever "grabbed my ear".

2011: with her supressed trauma.

Triggers reading

No, they have played on my conscience and stepped into the victim role. That is a far more effective and sustainable parenting method than using their hands.

You know, I wish mom would divorce dad. That she found her own apartment and the house in Sorunda had to be sold. And that it became a natural way to just clear out EVERYTHING. What would I keep?

2011: At work she performed a song

What-If-Letters to Little Brother

Wednesday 23rd of November 2011

Dearest Little Brother

I want to tell you about my struggle. I have had to fight for my rights to show that I am worthy of being treated so much better than our parents did.

I feel extremely humiliated and betrayed by our mother, disgusted with our father, and sad toward you. It was never my intention for our relationship to disappear/ fade away. I want you to know that you are worth fighting for. No one ever gave me that message.

My decision to cut my relationship with Mom and Dad does not mean that I want the same distance from you. All this will strengthen our relationship, and we can break the silence. I miss you and understand that once I am ready to tell you, it will be a lot for you to digest and take in.

Sister Gloomy

2011: in sign language which raised

What-If-Letters to Little Brother

Wednesday 30th of November 2011

Dear Little Brother,

Congratulations on your engagement. I'm happy for you, but it's just so ironic that one person gets engaged, and the other's relationship ends.

Unofficially, Dave and I broke up on the first day of Advent... Sunday.

When mom announced your engagement, I was stunned. I'm ashamed to admit it, but it was a confirmation that my life was falling apart.

That's what it felt like. You're not the only one getting engaged around me. Two of Dave's nephews are planning weddings for the summer of 2012.

I should be in that phase... planning my wedding.

How come you are there and I am not?

Big Sister Jealousy

PAPER-THIN

Thursday 8th of December 2011

Dear Little Brother,

I had my first meeting with Anna, the lawyer. She looked at the journal entries made by Social Services, the investigation that made it possible for me to leave home. She read the letter from my mother and listened to the audio recording I made of the last phone call with my father.

I don't know what this will lead to; I only have to tell the truth to live my life to the fullest.

Anna, the lawyer, was stunned by Dad's confession and apology. She says that things are looking up for a police report. Usually, you don't have this much evidence...

What I have in front of me now is how I can approach you with this.

It would be terrible to start a legal process without your knowledge.

I so hope you'll listen.

2011: Project with Barnombudsmannen

Triggers reading

'Alexandra's Room' VI:
Monday 23rd of January 2012

Honestly, I feel SO PROUD!

It feels like I've passed the point where I'm in high school left off in the book, now that we're on page 100!

FUCKING IVAN

The car is a curse that gives him the power to abduct Alexandra. The power to override his pleasure.

Destroyed…

My feeling at the moment of reading is: Oh no, Oh no

Here it comes, here it comes…

And then to express the abuse, Alexandra suffers in her own words.

2012.03.02: Presentations delivered

PAPER-THIN

The feeling of wanting to be picked up by mom

Wishing herself away from there

~ It will be over soon

~ He will stop soon

~ The incomprehension… Why is he doing this? Why is he implying that it's wrong?

 Feeling nauseous and uncomfortable

Uneasy feeling

2012.03.09: to ministers in charge.

Capsule Letter to Myself 6

To be opened on 31st of Oct 2023
Friday 26th of October 2012.

Dearest, most wonderful Annica.

It's been ages since I wrote you a Time Capsule letter, and what better time than now to do this as a strong Finish-off of Module 2?

This is a time of celebration. Dancing, reeling and honoring all I have done... all my aspects that are mine to enjoy, I embrace.

I am so in awe of everything I have done and the reality I am creating for myself.

This is so solemn that I don't know where to start...

My process has given me the courage to make new, empowering choices.

2012.03.22: She had reduced her

PAPER-THIN

I want to celebrate that I:

- Listening to my inner self. My realization of how I have treated myself when it comes to intimacy.

- Setting the boundaries that I don't want to have sex.

- Cut with my parents. STRONG BOUNDARY SETTING. I had not realized before how that relationship limited me… the extent it has oppressed me. Two weeks since I confronted my dad.

- I confronted my father for what he had done and I recorded the conversation!

- How I am taking much more responsibility for myself.

- The courage and will to attend body combat and boxing sessions.

- Atsub and the relationship with their staff. Tomorrow, it will be one year since I met them for the first time, and how it has developed me.

2012.03.22: working hours to study.

Capsule Letter to Myself 6

- The Children's Ombudsman. I have asked for my investigation and hold a treasure in my hands. It is as if I am ready to look deeper and walk (pilgrimage). And my story can help others, which is huge!

Cooking! Starting with home delivery of cooking supplies gave me incredible confidence, but I feel I slipped back into laziness when I canceled my subscription. I am feeling strong now to look for a better alternative.

- Finally, I took to heart the inner voice about going to the dentist. RESPONSIBLE.

- I have embraced the word 'adult.'

- I WENT DOWN IN TIME AT LINDEPARKEN... New opportunities opened up, and I came into contact with Skurugården.

On Cinnamon Bun Day, they gave me the responsibility to be a physical education teacher and the ultimate responsibility as an after-school coordinator! I have always experienced that level of responsibility, and I grew from it!

2012.03.22: This was an expensive

PAPER-THIN

However, what has changed the most in my life was performing at the student dinner with my sign song. Imagine that such a choice can open up a whole new reality. Just the fact that it opened up a contact with Mike. I'm not sure what the outcome will be, but my entire perspective on life changed when I performed at the student dinner with my sign song.

Imagine that the reality I took for granted, "This is what life should look like," has somehow limited me from an entire spectrum of unimaginable possibilities.

My Vision of how I got through my processing is anger, and the freedom that came from it (not least sexually and pleasurably) makes me grounded and motivated.

This is a time for detoxing. It feels incredibly liberating to have set aside tonight to declutter and clean. Freeing up space and energy… feeling clean. I am worthy of feeling good, enjoying being strong, and filled with love and energy.

2012.03.22: coping strategy.

Capsule Letter to Myself 6

This weekend, I am traveling to Skövde, and it will be so nice to get away for a while. But it is also tricky to reunite when I am a completely different person than the last time we saw each other—even though I am still ME.

I choose to have faith that everything is as it should be. I choose to observe how everything is right based on my process and how I can become the greatest expression of myself.

This is a time to exhale ...

Capsule Letter to myself 7

To be opened on 31st of October 2013
Wednesday 31st of October 2012

Dearest, most wonderful Annica,

My current situation ... well, it's a bit like I'm idling right now.

Last spring, the project with the Ombudsman for Children ended, and what a powerful experience that journey was. As you already know, the Ombudsman for Children (BO) is a government agency tasked with promoting and advancing children's rights and interests in Sweden, and the project during 2011/2012 was about hearing children who have been exposed to domestic violence.

Atsub invited me to share my story in this project, and it amazes me that this will affect Swedish law! And that my Story matters! It contributes and has a great impact on others in need! We made our presentations to the minister of justice, Beatrice Ask, and the minister of children and elderly, Maria Larsson.

2012.03.23: submit their rapport.

Capsule Letter to myself 7

My digital presentations were showcased on the news on 'Aktuellt' and shared with people in positional power during the Children's Rights Days.

The trip with the girls from the project was a nice ending. Taking part in all this is an incredible asset, and that I could influence it with my story is huge!

Unfortunately, this also resulted in me going into depression... I still take medication and feel low, but it's nothing compared to when I was at my worst.

I received support in finding a forensic psychologist, and today, I attended a psychotherapy group. We have met on nine occasions and are still in the process of getting to know each other.

March 2014 is our end date, and I can't even imagine where I will be then or how it will feel.

The relationship with my parents:
I haven't spoken to or seen my dad since I hung up the phone after the confrontational call, a tremendous liberation!

2012.04.24: 2 weeks 100% Sick leave

PAPER-THIN

My mom sent me a letter that I never answered.

I told Johan about the abuse!!! Then he immediately went out to Sorunda and put them against the wall!!!! He insisted it would be good to talk to Mom, so together with his beloved, we met Mom at their house at Thorildsplan.

That's the last time I saw her... and strangely enough, it felt like yesterday, even though it was well over a year ago. We are still friends on Facebook, and every month, she deposits 1500 SEK into my account. But we have no contact.

It was incredibly liberating to change my cell phone number. I'm independent, having my own phone with a number that is unknown to my parents, and I'm responsible for my bill. Despite my request to change the mobile number to mine, Dad extended the subscription (I get annoyed just thinking about it). Therefore, it felt incredibly beautiful to free myself and make this statement.

My medication increased my appetite, which I initially saw as only positive. Seeing the large portions on my plate motivated me just because I could :-).

2012.05.08 --> : Antidepressants

Capsule Letter to myself 7

Also, I feared I would feel hunger, but I felt the desire for food, a pleasant feeling! The weight gain also did not bother me at first.

But when the third person came up briefly to congratulate me on the pregnancy and wondered when the baby was due, it had to be enough. Already, the first time, it hurt me. My self-esteem then continued to plummet…

I tried Herbalife, this time for weight loss. The measurements are most important to me: slimmer shapes :-). Today is my first Herbalife day, and I look forward to seeing my results.

I am also waiting for the results of the health check I had last week. I am so proud that I took care of myself and brought myself to the blood test (it is hard to be so afraid of the syringe). I hope to get good guidance based on what the results show.

I just finished my first pole dance course, and my next starts next week. It feels super fun! I hope the feeling lasts!

When I try to approach someone, intimate relationships feel super messy. In a working relationship, it just gets crazy. However, I've tried a One-Night-Stand :-).

2012.05.08 --> : became her relief.

PAPER-THIN

It surprised me how nice it felt. I was lucky enough to meet a nice guy who showed great respect, so it actually felt nice even when we parted.

The relationship with Dave… We don't talk very often, but when we do, it's with warmth and great camaraderie. He's still one of my closest people… I often think of him during therapy sessions, and it's often with a great sadness that I haven't been able to meet him as I wanted to… or that he's been in trouble… that I haven't been able to communicate with him. It is extremely nice to have a distance from him, and that we are no longer together. It opens up the possibility of using the therapy in a way that would otherwise not be possible.

In 2010, we went to New York, and fulfilling a dream is one of the coolest things you can do! So, I continued to fulfill things I had been dreaming of for a long time. Something that also sped up this process was that Britt, who was in the kitchen at Lindeparken, suddenly passed away during the fall semester.

I felt that time was short and made my reservation at the Ice Hotel in Jukkasjärvi in March 2013. It's great to do something like that for my birthday!

Capsule Letter to myself 7

After checking around with people, I decided I wanted to travel with Dave. He is the one I feel most comfortable with, and it will be nice to experience the trip with him. It also feels like I will need a break in March.

I think a lot about what a police report would cause. Different scenarios, trial... prosecution... dad's reaction... mom's reaction... the feeling of "putting the lid on." Even though I repeatedly lift the lid or try to, it is still like the lid is put back on. Hush, hush, no one will know; close the doors, save the family's honor. Does a trial break this pattern? What happens inside me?

A big concern is how I will live at the same time. Already, I get stuck and have difficulty interacting with people. How will I feel once the carousel starts?

How do I wish I felt?

Free as a bird, jumping, skipping, playing, shining, singing, dancing, spontaneous, active, smiling, creative, making, lovely, beautiful, strong, fit, enjoying, tender, kind to myself and others, peaceful, loving.

Do I have to go through a trial to get there, or is accepting and forgiving myself enough?

2012.11.09: Filed the Police Rapport!

What-If-Letters to Mom

Wednesday 25th of September 2013

Okay, where do I start today?

I want you to know that it is reprehensible and unforgivable that you have not been there for me when I needed you most. It's horrible that you still cling to your powerlessness as if you couldn't live without it. I choose to let go of you because I will not allow myself to continue to be hurt by your betrayal. I deserve to be treated with respect and meaningful love, and I may protect my boundaries.

When you say you love me, it is just an empty word. It makes me sick to think about it. You don't know what love is. For me, loving someone means wanting to do everything for that person. Move mountains! You pretend the mountain doesn't exist.

Close your eyes and run away.

I want nothing from you anymore.

I never want to see you again.

2013.01.07: Hearing at the Police station

What-If-Letters to Mom

You have hurt and betrayed my innermost being... right down to the bone marrow.

It has distorted my worldview. Your betrayal has made me suspicious of the world around me and constantly on guard.

I choose not to waste any more energy on you because you are not worth it.

I need all my energy in my life.

I choose to change my life for the better, and I will find joy in doing so!

Saturday 28th of September 2013

You have ruined my life... and I have been left to survive on my own, fending for myself. "If you want something done, you have to do it yourself" is what you have taught me through your absence and self-imposed powerlessness.

And it hurts so much.

Mom, I was just a kid, and you didn't protect me or fight for me.

2013.02 - 2013.05: 100% Sick Leave

PAPER-THIN

I don't want you in my life because you don't want what's best for me. You have your sacrificial cardigan so well buttoned, with an oversized fluffy collar to hide in.

I've pointed to it.

I've tried to get you to take it off.

I've encouraged you to put it in the washing machine at least.

You're an energy thief; that's what you are.

I will not waste any more energy on you. You can sit there with your stale cardigan and feel sorry for yourself, and it disgusts me you are content with that.

You created a big hole in my life that can't be fixed. No matter what you do, you can't fix it. But the saddest thing is that you don't even try or want to.

Thursday, 3rd of October 2013

You know what, Mom?

2013.03.22: The proceeding was held

What-If-Letters to Mom

I am worth so much more. I don't want to hear your lame excuses that diminish you. Your clinging to them is the same as saying I wasn't worth more than that.

As if I didn't deserve to be protected by anger and rage.

I've had to fight that battle myself. I have done what any sensible mother would have done for her child. I brought the bastard to justice!

Naively, I thought it would help you open your eyes and realize what you can do, that it's not too late.

Your weakness has long been visible, and I feel so incredibly stupid today that I kept hoping.

I hoped my courage would strengthen and magically wake you from 100 years of sleep, breaking the spell. I hoped we would finally be happy, you and me.

Your betrayal is devastating. Together with you, my energy sinks in quicksand. It will never be you and me. I see it now with a broken heart.

2013.03.22: at court house!

PAPER-THIN

Wednesday 9th of October 2013

My value.

A fair reflection with others is that all my relationships are in my life for a reason. It is because I choose to spend time with those who uplift me and reflect on my values.

These people make me happy, want the best for me, and respect my boundaries. They see how valuable I am.

I can choose how I want to be treated.

Mom, you are not part of my life because you do not meet these criteria. "And it's your loss" that you have thrown away something as precious as your daughter for something as trivial as your chafing excuses, fears, and inaction are safe and familiar.

Thursday, 17th of October, 9.30 pm

I am not your cheerleader!

I will not condescend to pep you up.. I need all that energy to push myself to walk proudly and laugh with others.

2013.05 - 2013.08: 75% Sick Leave

What-If-Letters to Mom

You did not support me once on my long journey to stand up and reclaim what was my birthright to own.

Where was my cheerleader when I needed it most?

I am offended that you even update me on your own life.

Take care of your shit... don't dump it on me!

Tuesday 5th of November 2013

You know, I don't feel good.

I am more worried, nervous, and anxious than in a long time, trembling inside.

Dreaming about the end of the world and executions.

And I can't seem to get free because it's all inside... Under my skin.

Carrying a heavy heart and feeling depressed, heavy with sadness.

A sadness that does not want to come out.

22013.06.13: At ATSUB she met her,

Capsule Letter to myself 8

To be opened on 2nd of Nov 2014
Saturday 2nd of November 2013, 09.20 am

Dear Annica... Dear proud, confident, bubbly, playful, creative, spontaneous 29-year-old Annica,

It is strange because I do not know where I will be in a year. I am in a process of change, a shift where I am now leaving things behind to welcome new things, new goods, the middle of a process, a phase of fresh energy that I do not know what it will bring. It's exciting to think that you have all those answers.

I still haven't read the letter that 27-year-old Annica has "sent" to me. Opening it now, a list of thoughts pops up... :-).

5 A4 pages and a photo!

2013.06.13: mom for the first time

Capsule Letter to myself 8

The journey with the Children's Ombudsman, the achievements of Maria Larsson and Beatrice Ask. Shit, how cool to read the words of someone who just experienced it. So powerful :-).

Depression, group therapy. 1500 SEK, own mobile number, weight, pole dancing, intimate relationships. Wow, my One-Night-Stand :-).

Dave

"Putting the lid on,"

The short skirt felt, after a while, not as important, dear Annica. Those were the ones I performed in and that's what was in the photo. No, I actually donated it along with other outgrown summer clothes to Mary, who went to Ghana this fall. Nice that they can bring joy to others. I took a wardrobe planning course and I got a jolt to build a basic wardrobe and took to heart what they said about letting go of the clothes you don't use. Once you've reached your ideal weight and can get into that garment again, you're worthy of new garments, anyway.

2013.06.13: since the brake in 2011

PAPER-THIN

Weight? I think it's linked to my medication, which I still have as support. I switched to using Herbalife as a healthy breakfast and it also provided a more stable everyday life. Over the past year, I have gone through a huge process and journey where weight was not a priority.

It has only been a few months since I became interested in spending time at the gym (in Skärholmen) and measuring my progress on weight, BMI, etc, again.

It is nice to see that I have lost four centimeters around my stomach since the 12th of September 2013. It will be fun to see if the muscle mass has changed somewhat the next time I stand on the scale. Otherwise, there is hardly any hard training, but the most important thing is wellness right now.

My outstanding process! It is remarkable that in my last letter, I can reflect upon what my actions are resulting in. I dared to stand up for myself, and I went ALL-IN.

I FILED A POLICE REPORT!

I WENT THROUGH A LEGAL PROCESS AND TRIAL!

2013.07: That summer she joined her

Capsule Letter to myself 8

I GOT PROOF THAT I WAS RIGHT...

A CONFESSION AND A CONVICTION

A process that took six months!

- Police report November 2012
- The damages were in my account in May 2013.

Life was on hold during this time, just as many people described it before me. I took full-time sick leave when my dad was arrested in February. I couldn't go to work anymore.

I've had a hard time relating to my sick leave, but it becomes so clear now that I'm explaining it. I'm proud that I dared to press the PAUSE BUTTON to clarify and correct something I don't want to carry for the rest of my life. Finally, someone will hold him accountable for what he has done. It is his shame to bear.

I replace his shame with my pride that I have made it right, that I have done what the adult world did not do for me as a four-year-old and 18-year-old.

2013.07: friends on their trip to Cuba.

PAPER-THIN

I have fought for the rights and self-esteem of these girls. I am proud to send them peace.

"Putting the lid on" is a term I haven't used in ages. Reading the phrase in my last letter made me jump because I had almost forgotten it. I can't relate to it anymore, mainly because I got a confession and because the legal process/trial really made it visible.

It's great to know that B1's parents know everything. And that my parents have understood it. It's great that my mother can no longer live in Sorunda, that she can no longer close her eyes. On the 1st of January, she moves to a two-room apartment in Ösmo. It's unbelievable that something I've dreamed of for most of my childhood is actually becoming a reality.

It is probably the case that a trial does not fit in a box to put a lid on it...

Or is it the conviction that doesn't fit into a box?

The confession?

2013.07: She fell in love with it all!

Capsule Letter to myself 8

However, I can relate with my grandfather, for example. I never call him because I don't want to be forced to pretend that my father is a saint. In contact with my grandfather, it is as if my struggle never existed or was in vain.

Even when I've run into my cousin, the worry has hung in the air. In these situations, there is still a "lid".

Since the verdict came, my mother has stopped depositing money, and that is extremely nice. We have met a few times at Atsub, and it is now so clear that her process is hers. It is a relief to stop hoping for her. So nice!

Then came the news of her move. (It's also nice, but I don't really know where to go with that information.)

The group therapy was a tremendous support throughout my legal process. There is a lot I can discuss there, a forum for understanding what I'm going through. Something I can't find anywhere else.

Well, Atsub, of course! But there, you don't get the same depth of reflection from others.

2013.07: That's why she'd revisit.

PAPER-THIN

We now have our end date in the group 2014-03-26 v.13.

It feels strange that there will be a time in my life (soon, too) when I can put my processing behind me. It's a tantalizing thought ... which still feels unreal.

Last letter, I had taken my first pole dancing course! It was so much fun! I continued with a course and a half more until I pressed the pause button. I also went stretching and tried FYS. I long to return to this and look forward to taking it up again after completing group therapy.

The trip to the Ice Hotel in Jukkasjärvi was fantastic! It was days before the trial, and traveling with Dave then was priceless! Fulfilling a dream and focusing on something so cool really lifted me. It was magical!

Another dream fulfilled is my participation in this year's Rag Doll Day, a public gathering that Atsub is hosting! I rode in the motorcycle convoy and got to hold the rag doll when we entered Medborgarplatsen!

2013.08 - 2013.12: She enjoyed a

Capsule Letter to myself 8

It is enormous to realize something that I have been looking forward to in my process: a Pride parade after a trial and conviction with damages. I also read poems and gave a pep talk before the trip!

The trip to Cuba was not to realize a dream… it was to treat myself to something bigger after all the hard things I had been through. It was to get away and experience the sun and warmth in a place where the concept 'Beach 2013' did not exist. :-) Well, that was actually what decided that I still said YES to follow John, Helena, and their daughter there. I did not feel comfortable with my figure before, but I did not worry for a second while there. It was rather my paleness that I found difficult.

I had a wonderful time! Being in a place with so much joy, warmth, desire, and curiosity was so cool that I'm going back this New Year to visit Pepito, a Cuban guy that I fancy.

My new journey is also for the sake of my well-being. It is a developing journey that, for a part, challenges me to let go of the need for control and to be in the present.

2013.08 - 2013.12: Spanish course!

PAPER-THIN

Last summer I got from Vallagränd 19 all the way to Havana airport with two plane changes (London + Toronto) completely on my own! I grew enormously from that!

This time around, it's more challenging. It's about managing the journey there, a three-week stay (without English, interpreter, or the like), and returning home! Can you imagine what I will grow from this!!!

I have almost finished my two semesters of Spanish at Medborgarskolan and have had the attitude that it is not enough. But if you compare what I learned last trip with what I learned now, it makes my three weeks easier.

What about intimate relationships?

It was challenging to tell Dave about Pepito, or rather strange. We were in the cottage, and then his mum naturally helped us make our beds in separate bedrooms. Nice, but strange. We sometimes talk on the phone and can hug a little longer when we see each other. It's like being in unfamiliar territory.

2013.12.04: Through her mom she

Capsule Letter to myself 8

That he testified means so much to me. That his testimony didn't match my truth meant even less because my attitude was always that all the truth would come out, regardless. His honesty and presence meant everything!

Dave is and remains an important part of my life. He understands me in a way that others do not because we share so much history/memories.

Mike. Lord God, all the tours with this man…

June:

- At the Lindeparken R.I.P. party, we made out in the schoolyard and in the dark at YTD.

- After work, make out all the way to the bus stop.

August:

- Talked about the vacation trip to Cuba.

October:

- Tube crawl → followed him home.

2013.12.04: got the opportunity to

PAPER-THIN

And everything is in between when my inner self goes on a roller coaster of how I should react, behave, etc...

During the last tube crawl, he made me open my eyes to how men see me. Observing and reflecting is scary because it's new, unknown territory or something that feels my limits at home with him. And not to end up in shame and neediness by saying no to penetration/sex.

My 'no' is being respected, which is extremely important!

And to see him enjoy, feel it... it did something to my self-confidence. Respecting my 'no' did something to my self-esteem. Not long after my "Wow, I can't believe I'm getting this close!" a new thought emerged: "Wow, I can't believe I WANT to get this close!"

So, dear future Annica.

It would be so cool to know where this relationship is in your life :-). Will I experience passionate sex with this man? Do I want that...? ;-).

2013.12.04: collect all her remaining

Capsule Letter to myself 8

Today, I don't want that, but somehow, I wish my process takes me to a deep inner self-esteem, an unparalleled confidence, an appearance I appreciate and show love... That I am radiant, bursting with joy, energy, and confident to live my outstanding life. Let's meet on a whole new level.

Pepito... well... where do I start?

I don't know; I have gained some perspective since coming home from our visit this summer. I was afraid of being exploited for profit, but as time passed, perhaps I unintentionally was the one who exploited him. It was not for his sake that I was traveling, but for my own. And that's how it should be. It's healthy to focus on one's process and well-being.

I hardly know people there. My next journey will be an experience in a series of experiences, an adventure. Taking a trip like this is a rare opportunity. It is not something that everyone can do. I would regret so much if I missed this and lived it to the fullest. Only after this trip can I know how I actually feel about Pepito.

2013.12.04: boxes that was stored in

PAPER-THIN

I think a lot about who I will meet next time. Sandy has flagged that a friend of hers could be an interesting date :-).

I would like to be with someone who understands me. Meeting with Pepito is so exciting and challenging on so many levels. We live in two completely different worlds: culturally, technically developed, linguistically, phases of life, and dreams; all this makes me develop in my encounter with him. But no matter how much Spanish I learn or Swedish he could learn... we will never fully understand each other. I already know that.

Even the fantasy of being with a deaf/sign language guy who helps me develop my sign language skills will be tempered because we will still not fully understand each other. Or maybe sign language would work? An interpreter? Hmm... I'll have to fidget about that a bit more.

This year, I have been thinking a lot about finances.

- Made a list of where the money goes

- save the receipt app

2013.12.04: their basement. Most

Capsule Letter to myself 8

- Read the book 'How all Swedes can become millionaires' and 'How to have a rich life as a pensioner'.

- Attended the lecture 'A richer life.'

But above all, I have thought a lot about the damages I fought for.

Hence, there is an internal dialog about housing. I enjoy my small rental apartment at Proventum, but if there is something I should allocate a sum for, it is a condominium.

I have submitted an expression of interest in the BRF Argos project Peab is planning. I have not gone to the bank and asked for a mortgage because I do not know the conditions, fees, etc. An apartment in the Old Haninge municipal building will also increase in value. I think that in a year, I will still live in my cozy apartment here at Vallagränd 19,.... but maybe I have bought a condominium that is being completed, with occupancy in the winter of 2015.

2013.12.04: importantly, she ceased

PAPER-THIN

Miranda is part of my life, and I intend to maintain that relationship. Taking care of someone else's cat for a while is the ultimate way to have a cat :-) All the best without responsibility long-term and financially. So, I don't think I want my own cat in the next few years.

I plan to reintroduce the home delivery of food supplies, the Inspiration Box, in my life. After completing the Spanish course, I will introduce the first box on the 25th of November.

It would be fun if even the time at the gym felt more interesting.

I went for an IPL hair removal treatment. How was the result? Do you feel satisfied? Is it nice not to keep shaving? I'm hoping to feel smooth and fresh :-).

What dreams have I fulfilled that have given me energy?

What new dreams has it made room for?

Which projects/creations have kept me company?

Capsule Letter to myself 8

WHAT DOES MY WORK SITUATION LOOK LIKE?

I have now made up to 50% from being on sick leave. I long to work 100% ... not because I want to, but to feel that I can and feel good about that well-being. The thought excites me :-).

I dream of working extra as a companion. I wonder where I will be in a year!

In conclusion, I would like to say a few words:

I advise you to continue ordering the calendar from www.personligalmanacka.se. It's exciting to see your dreams realized every time you pick it up!

I want to introduce something new: to end the year with a summary as a photo book from Önskefoto. Highlights of the year and dreams fulfilled. I have just started working on my first one, a summary of my process during my three years at Atsub!

I have attended an online photo book workshop and signed up for another one for even more inspiration :-).

2013.12.04: Grandpa on his deathbed

PAPER-THIN

I wish you all the best! Are you inspired to live life to the fullest and realize new dreams? I send you an intention to laugh and play, dance, make new creations, jump in many piles of leaves, express yourself with sign language, enjoy closeness and intimacy, set boundaries where needed and protect them, trust people, and the universe wants the best for you.

There are no limits to what you can achieve in your life. Dare to reach for what you desire.

Because you are truly worth it!

BIG HUGS

2013.12.25: That same winter, she

Dear Diary 14

Tuesday 17th of June 2014

Dear Annica/ Myself & my fears

Yesterday, I received the acceptance letter. The Living Workshop has admitted me to a two-year teaching program in art and design. The first day of school starts on the 25th of August at 10 am.

I was sitting in the craft room at work when I saw that the email had arrived. I was shaking when I opened it and got all teary-eyed when I read it. It was a relief, but it was shocking and felt unreal.

It still does.

Somehow, I will take this course, while the uncertainty of its impact on my value scares me enormously!

2013.12.25: revisited Cuba singing.

PAPER-THIN

While I know that I have the potential to develop tremendously in leadership, especially in an area I am passionate about, something tells me that the short 'Desire to Create' course the school also provides might be better suited. One semester later, it's over. But I don't want it to end. I want to study for two years at Södra Stockholm Folkhögskola.

Desire, community, creativity, and inspiration are also present in the long course. I look forward to finding security in trusting the process, letting go of the need for control, learning to play, laugh, and welcome change because that's what it means to receive instructions that change/build upon the previous instruction during the creative process.

And to create together, learn from others, and dare to meet the eyes of others.

This is going to be GREAT!

PS. And yes, I am in love with Tony :-)

2014: Gradualy she increased her

Capsule Letter to Myself 9

To be opened on X-mas Eve 2015!
Sunday 2nd of November 2014, 2.10 pm

Annica, it will be so exciting to finally read the letter you wrote a year ago.

Sitting with pen in hand, ready to make notes while reading …

The last letter was apparently on five A4 pages and with a photo… This is two letters! One has 12 A5 sheets written on the front and back, and the second letter is another such sheet!!!! Shit, pommes frites, (like the saying goes) :-).

I have had an incredible journey; that's my spontaneous reaction. When you reach your ideal weight, you are worthy of new clothes, that feels inspiring :-)

And dear contemporary Annica… I'm glad you were interested in going to the gym a year ago. Even though it is not exactly where I hang out today, it still laid some kind of foundation for continued training. THANK YOU.

2014: working hours, but realised

PAPER-THIN

Even today, I desire to stand on the staff scale and see my development. Since I started running PT Deluxe at Sthlmpole and devoted more time to dance, I have actually seen a marked difference. And I feel a marked difference! It's outstanding!

However, as you say, it is important for wellness, something I easily neglect.

When you wrote your letter, you had stopped dancing.

I tried Pole Rookie, Polestar, and 'Pole Addict' before my hiatus kicked in before I pressed my pause button. Wow, that was an important reminder that it was a conscious and active choice!

I also did stretching sessions and tried FYS.

Since I took up the dance again, I have run Pole-Superstar (which was added as a new level) (went it twice) Pole-Addict and is now in my second round of Pole-Master. Have also gone to Pole-Dancer, some stretching.

Capsule Letter to Myself 9

It took off properly this summer when I chose that summer 2014 would be a pole dance summer :-) I exchanged sunburn for bruises and intensive courses. And since last fall / late summer, I have gone to PT Deluxe with Anna. It is probably one of the best decisions, actually. I found so much motivation and have a different way of thinking about the diet. This will be the 10th week. During my break, I also spent a lot of time with Ida Naprapat. Fantastic. I would not have reached here without her support, actually.

While we're discussing dancing, I can continue to write a bit about it before I continue to read your letter. I have just gone through a process and realized how important it is for me to keep pole dancing as a love boost and source of energy.

With the training I am now attending, Living Workshop (which I did not know about a year ago!) I have learned things such as

"The least amount of energy for the most amount of results."

"Don't Worry Be Happy."

2014: creative education

PAPER-THIN

"Dare to trust the present... that everything will work out... and I can safely let go of my need for control."

"We do not strive for perfection."

I saw all this as an opportunity to take advantage of dance and thus signed up for the audition held before the 2014 Club Championships.

Our mentor showed us you can spice up your life by creating projects. I made dance a project.

The first step was at the level where all the pieces were, and I took part in the audition! I feel completely satisfied and proud that I did it, and it felt great!

My entire attitude was to go there and show what I've learned without performance... and it turned into a bit of mini-choreography after all. Super cool!

Capsule Letter to Myself 9

Audition and KM were different things for me. As soon as KM accepted me, the no-performance approach transformed into something else: it became goal-oriented, performance-oriented, scrutinized, and evaluated… by myself, I must add.

Something individual sad replaced group togetherness, excitement, and loneliness. It required a lot of back-and-forth, but I also feel confident in my decision to decline to take part in KM today. It is a relief, and I look forward to maintaining the love of my training and leisure interests.

Seeing KM as an audience member and spectator will also be fun.

Tuesday 4th of November 2014, 8.55 am

My outstanding process

Dear Annica, you are truly amazing! What a struggle you have gone through!

2014 - 2016: During these years the

PAPER-THIN

I reflect on the fact that the confession and the trial make "put the lid on" superfluous and that it is not in my vocabulary. You say that it still exists in the relationship with Grandpa and your cousin.

My grandfather passed away in the spring, and it felt good that I had the courage to visit him one last time… even though it was terribly painful. What do you say to someone you know you won't see again? *tears* At least not in this life.

It took tremendous courage to attend the funeral. I had Dave's parents, and Helena with me. Mom was late, but she sat with us, as she had said. And the emotions went on a roller coaster. It was so humiliating to sit at the back among the mourners and see those I once called family sitting in the first row of benches. The absurdity of being in that situation at all. And a tremendous grief over my grandfather's passing.

Capsule Letter to Myself 9

My presence opened up for a nice meeting with my cousins. Actual tears fell at the first eye contact when they turned around and, with a smile (mixed with sadness), mimes "Hello." It felt enormous and the meeting at the funeral opened the door for me to go down and visit my cousin this summer. It Feels like we are building something now :-).

I never had eye contact with Dad, but it was really powerful that I caught up with him and Johan, who quickly rushed ahead of everyone else towards the parish hall.

I was only a few meters behind their backboards when my sister-in-law got my brother to turn around so I could say goodbye. She then put her arms around my dad and continued in. It was absolutely crazy, and I feel so proud that I stood there straight back!

It's also great that I did the right thing to meet my brother in his grief. If I had not taken the initiative, we would never have seen each other there.

PAPER-THIN

To focus on my grandfather, I can say that his passing gave me a kind of peace. Today, I never feel guilty about Sorunda. I did then. I always felt conflicted. Guilt that I never went there, that I never called, that I couldn't be myself or relax.

Another powerful experience after my grandfather passed away was dreaming about him. He really shone. He was his old fun-loving self, bubbly as ever.

He repeated or emphasized the message "Finally," and how great it was that the phone call finally took place. It was an incredibly beautiful and intense dream, a warm hearted encounter.

When I woke up, I knew he was referring to the conversation with my dad that I recorded on tape. That conversation became evidence, and that was what led to the conviction. And I know that Grandpa now understands why I was absent. Between us, we have forgiven and reconciled. I think of him with great love.

Capsule Letter to Myself 9

You said it still existed in the relationship with Grandpa and your cousin. Believe it or not, I have actually built a relationship with her too! Much thanks to one of my classmates, who is a close friend of my cousin.

You could say that the lid is on, together with her, but I still do not use that term. I've decided that it doesn't have to affect my relationship with my cousin. Family ties have felt more important because I have so few.

They invited me to join their Vista group, which basically means they meet and do crafts. The first meeting is tomorrow, and it will be interesting to see where it goes.

My mom and I have been texting occasionally since recently. We had a long break since the funeral. I mentioned seeing her on a craft day at her house, but there was no new date. Johan sent an SMS and told me he would like to come by then and see her. We have not heard a word since the funeral, and suddenly, this came. Turns out there's a baby on the way. I'm going to be an aunt in June.

PAPER-THIN

Strangely, I feel more overwhelmed than happy. I will land in it, eventually. Outstanding, dear future Annica... How does it feel now? You who have already met them? I hope that you have found an approach and clarity in the relationship so that you can feel safe and comfortable in your relationship with the child. I do not, under any circumstances, want to be in the same room as my father, and I hope everyone respects this.

The time when I can put this active processing behind me has come... and it feels fantastic!

This trip to Cuba is unbelievable! I went there on my own over New Year without knowing the language, with the knowledge I studied at Medborgarskolan and Helena just a text message away, and spent three fantastically rewarding weeks with Pepito. It was absolutely crazy! And I did it! I encountered many cultural clashes and new experiences while feeling so good from the sun and heat.

It's absolutely crazy that Yoshua and I changed places while I was on sick leave. Oh my God! I had also repressed that, but I got reminded of it now. It's very brave and very rewarding!

Capsule Letter to Myself 9

Haha, intimate relationships; how many pages did I write about it in the last letter, five and a half A5 pages? You asked where I am in the relationship with Mike :-). I think it is on an excellent de-dramatized level, but somehow, we will always have a special bond with each other. He opened my eyes to how other men looked at me on the tube crawl. It was the first party that Tony was at. Nothing happened there, but in hindsight, even he showed interest.

Mike has meant a lot to me, and the relationship between him and Dawe settled comfortably when Tony and I started dating and showing interest in each other. I felt very comfortable there and then. I have no desire for a passionate relationship with Mike, and I was thrilled that he, as a nice colleague, contacted me when events happened as I wished.

I still wish to reach deep inner self-esteem and unparalleled self-confidence, an appearance I appreciate and show love for. I am radiant, bursting with joy, energy, and confidence to live my outstanding life.

And maybe we can meet on a whole new level???

2014 - 2016: made her stonger and

PAPER-THIN

A year ago, that last sentence probably meant passionate, hot, and wild sex. When I read the sentence today, it meant something completely different. It's an intellectual level, respectful, slow, reverent.

Wednesday 31st of December 2014, 11:25 am

And all meetings/relationships are small steps in that process.

2014 was the year I started dating. Tony was a very important part of that. Even though it didn't last, it was extremely respectful.

Then, I joined the Tinder dating app, which was an experience in itself that challenged me to be who I wanted to be. Gökhan, can you say that we were each other's pleasant pastime?

I wanted sex and passion… but I realized that passion is something other than sporadic sexual encounters in a relationship that doesn't develop.

Ferdi showed me that it's perfectly okay to go out for coffee without kissing at the end of the date. This was perhaps one of the most valuable experiences.

2014 - 2016: more joyful than ever.

Capsule Letter to Myself 9

Robban, I picked up on the dance floor at the salsa club and gave out my number myself! I have been out once since then... and now we sporadically text about dancing sometimes. Alfons was a brief fascination at work.

Tahir was an unexpected encounter.

(my number is six, by the way)

Regardless, they are all part of my process.

And somehow, I deeply wish that I was in love before the next time I have sex. That sex will be deeper and more meaningful to the man I have feelings for. A man who also has feelings for me and that we can create magic together.

The love that just "strikes you" and that I can't resist... that I don't want to resist but welcome with open arms.

It feels difficult to mention Bastian here... because I want to let go of hopes and expectations. I want to be. And that's exactly how it is right now... we just are... for five hours a day on Messenger!... and the relationship is deepening all the time... just by being ourselves.

2014 - 2016: She finally got her

PAPER-THIN

We have written to each other (on Tinder and Messenger) every day since last summer and Messenger since November, and on Saturday, we will meet for the first time. I'm going to Växjö! Exciting and yet so obvious.

No, I choose not to analyze or go into it… it will be so much fun, Annica, to see how you feel in all this. Tell me how it all went :-).

We have a lot of fun together on Messenger … click intellectually and spiritually … (want to click on all levels)

I still live in my studio apartment at Vallagränd 19. I haven't invested in a condominium, even though I know that I have earmarked the money for one. I'm questioning it. Will I ever want to live in a condominium? Yes, probably. Otherwise, the money has gone on Cuba trips and a lot of dancing. Now that I've started studying, I've picked up pots there instead of cutting back on my standard of living, to put it bluntly.

I have been thinking about finances a lot now, too. I have even made annual summaries / monthly summaries in 2014 and long to plan with a budget as well… not just evaluations.

Capsule Letter to Myself 9

Miranda is still a part of my life.

I have also just started as a companion, which feels great.

IPL stopped feeling important. It's not completely hair-free, but there has been a significant reduction, which feels good.

It hurt so much and clashed with the fact that I went to the naprapath and wanted to feel soft. Maybe it's something to take up again eventually, but one area at a time! Not all at once, like last time.

That I started studying at the Living Workshop Educator program is one of the best things I have done! Partly because I'm doing something 100%! Big!

But it is not mainly at Lindeparken. That place would have suffocated me if I hadn't made a change. Actually…

On Friday, I'll be working a holiday at KTT. It'll be my first eight-hour shift in ages. I can't remember when I last worked full-time :-).

PAPER-THIN

Will not make a "big deal" of it. Just go there and have fun.

It will be a good intro for the summer vacation. It will also be full-time for several weeks. I need that income.

This year, by the way, I'm going to take out the contraceptive stick. Good luck with that.

Monday 5th of January 2015, 10.15 pm

I choose to end this letter like I did the last one.

Because it is a given.

Dear beloved, fantastic, amazing Annica.

I wish you all the best!

That you have gained new inspiration to live life fully and realized new dreams.

2014 - 2016: was also active as the

Capsule Letter to Myself 9

I send you an intention to laugh and play, dance, make new creations, jump in many piles of leaves, express yourself with sign language, enjoy closeness and intimacy, set boundaries where needed and cherish them, trust people, and trust that the universe wants the best for you.

There are no limits to what you can achieve in life, and it is my vision that you have the courage to pursue your desires.

You are definitely worth it.

I wish for you to shine your brightest

BIG HUGS

This is a turning point in life.

And anything can happen now.

How exciting to experience 2015

2014 - 2016: associations cashier.

Dear Diary 15

Friday 12th of January 2024

It's about revealing the facade that no longer serves me.

The diaries have been a central starting point for my writing. But since all of them had been in place here in my mother-in-law's apartment since my last visit, I felt like I needed to bring something else tangible with me.

I packed up the binder with the documents from the trial and all my almanacs from 2012 to 2022 to continue with my life.

They held the trial on the 22nd of March, 2013 and announced the verdict on the 28th of March, 2013.

There is an inherent desire for a holistic perspective, a kind of understanding of what happened, to reconcile with it. I want to say "Rest in peace" to that part of me, so that it can strengthen me and feel whole.

2016: She met her kitten Glitter

Dear Diary 15

Throughout my life, I have felt 'broken,' and I have repeatedly tried to fix myself in the materialistic world with all kinds of courses and treatments. I haven't been willing/able/ready to go through my process. I've instead tried to get around it by resorting to external, tangible solutions.

Immersing yourself in a ten-session spa treatment to eliminate your warts is fantastic! You feel you are doing something concrete to correct them, and you feel good, and it pays off.

Afterward, the wallet is empty... and inside me, the feeling is also emptiness. Despite living on my illusion that "I fix myself," the remaining feeling inside is that I am "broken."

The instinct kicks in and takes extra steps to "fix myself"...

IPL hair removal treatment, LPG treatment for connective tissue massage and clearing out waste products, decluttering my home and clearing out stagnant energies, going to the gym and mastering the different exercises on the pole in my pole dancing class...

2016 - 2019: Therapy bi-weekly

PAPER-THIN

Create my ideal wardrobe, patch, and mend my clothes. Clearing out, organizing, structuring, and sorting.

It becomes a kind of addiction that each time leaves a bitter aftertaste and sadness that I can't get rid of, the feeling of not being "whole" and that nothing I indulge in is permanent.

Saturday 13th of January 2024

I thought about the timeline... What is it that I want to cover?

Places I've lived in?

People I told?

What is it I want clarity about?

Sunday 28th of January 2024, 11.30 am

I am sitting at See You At Work, the office landscape (a soundproof box). It's so harmonious somehow to be here, and it feels so luxurious that we have this opportunity for a few more weeks before our subscription expires.

2017: Found a Four Leaf Clover

Dear Diary 15

I've had a brutal headache all morning, and it almost doesn't seem worth spending 4 hours on a Sunday on this writing. I prefer an entire week of the writing process, compared to jumping in and out of a writing process where it takes energy and hurts, remembering, feeling, and trying to describe in the best way possible.

WHAT HAPPENED TO ME?

WHY DID IT HAPPEN?

WHY DIDN'T ANYONE PROTECT ME?

UNDERSTAND THE TIMELINE... in what order did everything happen?

LAND IN NEW INSIGHTS

CLARITY & CLOSURE → REALIZE MOODBOARD

Sunday 4th of February 2024, 11.30 am

Back at See You At Work...

2018: Went on a rollercoaster ride

PAPER-THIN

It's so frustrating to jump in and out of the writing process. Now that I sit down and try to get started structuring and organizing everything I've written, it really feels like starting from scratch.

Sunday 11th of February 2024, 3.30 pm

I don't know what's wrong with me... Jumpy, hard to interact with people... feeling stressed, stomach ache. Something in the conversation makes me shake... like I'm weird.

Have become wrapped up in memories that make me nostalgic, but not...

Writing in a notebook... like the ones you can see journalists using. reminds me of the feeling of holding a notebook in my hand in 1992.

Writing with different colored gel pens, just like in high school.

I feel sad and depressed... tired.

Even the reviewer in me, looks at my words with a disgusted look... nothing flows, and everything feels blue...

2019.07.18: Her daughter was born.

Dear Diary 15

"You know what, darling? I think writing your book here at home might do you some good."

My husband said it as a warm and honest observation. One of his greatest strengths is giving input without judgment where I'm most stuck and somehow magically untie the knots that keep me stuck.

I initially flinched at his words but understood what he meant.

"You no longer have to walk around thinking your story is tainting your life. You can now write the book while sitting at your desk in our bedroom. It might even do you some good."

I had previously explained that I prefer to write in a place other than my home, partly for privacy but also to avoid bringing the emotional labor of writing my book into our home.

We had it brought into our home. Honestly, it's pretty heavy right now to write. I've compiled it, but so much is still missing.

I don't know where on the timeline to start, so let's just try...

2020.10.21: First date with David

PAPER-THIN

My husband, David, and I met through Tinder, a dating app. My daughter had just turned 1, and I had recently ended my relationship with her biological father. The last three years with him had been very turbulent. Life was like an involuntary roller coaster ride during this time. I didn't feel comfortable just being on the peaks or the valleys, doing my best to cope without being able to figure out when the next turn would take me by surprise.

So when I created my profile on Tinder as a single parent of a young child, I hoped to find love and stability. A man with whom my daughter and I could share our lives.

And there he was, "Mr. Davisin."

His photos showed a handsome man standing on stage, talking to a large female audience. I super-liked him and got a little tingle in my stomach as we started our chat conversation. I often sat in the local cafe and enjoyed our coffee and conversation.

Dear Diary 15

I appreciated that we had written to each other long before our first date. It was a marvelous month for me, but looking back at the chat history, I realize that it was only a week of writing before we decided on our first date.

Sunday 25th of February 2024, 5.30 pm

Feel it; be curious.

It's all about the energies and the inner dialog.

There's no right or wrong; it doesn't have to be in a certain way.

The book will lead to conversations!

I could have prompts in the book.

It might even be expressive to include the timeline as a visual thread throughout the book.

Do I want to include a QR code?

Perhaps I could add exercises in the book for the reader to develop with me?

2022.07.18: Got engaged at home

PAPER-THIN

I'm getting stuck in my writing, like having a scratch in the groove of an old fashion vinyl record.

I read out loud what I've written and try to move on to where it stops again and again.

"So maybe you need an alternative approach. It sounds like that's what you just said,". This new approach was so obvious when Jean, my coach and editor, said it. Just like when he reminded me it's called "Writer's Block," not "Writers Stop."

Instead:
1. Write what you want to say, and there will be a structure…

2. You then tell the story…

3. And finally, summarize what you've just said. Sort of.

I guess the thing is that I "don't want to tell." I want to be done already…

And yes, now realize the twist and how I can use it to my advantage. "I want to be done already, and therefore, I want to tell!"

2023.01.11: Got married @ Chou Chou

Dear Diary 15

Thursday 23rd of May 2024, 7.30 pm

"If you get to the finish line, the journey is complete.
Is it possible that you get more out of healing than being healed?"

"What occurs when the book gets published ... is there a fear that the processing would cause having to spend time with your father?"

Yes, there's something in what my husband put into words by asking me those questions. Even if I mentally know that forgiveness does not mean I have to spend time with my father, there's still a part of me deep within that's having that fear. But by forgiving, I'm not saying "yes, please" to having a relationship.

Instead, I'm saying "Yes, please" to living my life fully without having to drag around the toxic energy of hiding my story and how that has impacted my different life aspects.

I'm forgiving and saying "Yes, please" to living my Mood board, fulfilling the areas where I've not yet allowed myself to shine my brightest.

PAPER-THIN

I'm forgiving and moving on, strengthened by the process of writing this book and the insight that forgiveness is beyond our human struggles in life. It's a reconnection with our true selves and that we're part of something larger than ourselves as a collective.

After going through my journals, letters, and struggles, I am now able to reflect on what paths in life led me to… It has helped me to look beyond myself instead of locking myself in my own Ego and saying, "No, thanks," to having a relationship with my dad.

Because the thing is, that perspective is just not relevant any longer. It's important to live life fully on my own terms, to live my life passionately as a way to serve others. These are precisely my next steps forward, and I will anchor this within myself.

As a first step, my husband and I are packing our backpacks to visit Amsterdam. It's an adventure that will shake me up, but mainly an enjoyable way to celebrate his 40th birthday and a well-deserved celebration of my accomplishments.

Cheers!

2024: Planning a book release party

EPILOGUE

Thursday 13th of June 2024

Beloved Mum!

When I started compiling this book just over a year ago, it was out of an inner longing to reconcile with my story, to anchor myself and be able to live my life to the fullest.

My work brought my book project to life when I met Jean Dorff and The Empowering Story Program. As you already know, David and I help instructors create and sell their online courses. I am so fortunate to be inspired by and support so many outstanding coaches and course creators who are truly making the world a better place simply by following their passion and thriving by helping others.

Jean helps women to heal from sexual abuse by writing and publishing their story as a book in 90 days or less, or he'll continue working with you 1:1 for free until you do.

PAPER-THIN

My worldview was overturned for a different reason when he entered our lives. I had long since finished my therapy and treatment, convinced that I was now "done" and would live life and play with my newfound David, without having to be bothered by my history.

David frequently told me about our new client, Jean, without me even being ready to "take in" what he was saying. My ears just "switched off," and my body went into flight mode. It was simply too scary to cope with my story in this new phase of my life, and it took me off guard. Once I realized it, this became an important signal that I had more layers to work on and that it was time for it.

Inside me, I always knew that a book needed to be written, and it just made sense to do that together with Jean.

I see now that this book is mainly about my relationship with you, Mum. Although we still haven't realized complete reconciliation, I'm proud to dedicate our story to my daughter, your granddaughter.

Thank you for the letter you wrote to me in October 2011, shortly after I cut contact with you and Dad by phone.

Epilogue

That was 13 years ago (I was 26), and I couldn't reply to you in all the turmoil that was then. It probably wouldn't have benefited either of us in that situation. Today, I am 39 years old, and I am grateful that since then, in action, you have shown me I am important. It was not another empty word in a letter, but the starting point for our great relationship.

We met at ATSUB and talked with counselling. I remember it as difficult and rigid… but extremely important.

One of the biggest breakthroughs was getting your own place. As long as you lived with Dad, it was impossible to rebuild your relationship with me.

I also remember my grandfather's funeral and how incredibly scared I was to go into the church. I sat in the car with my friends for the longest time… and you were late.

When it was time to enter the church, I had no idea where to sit, and I am so grateful that my friend took the initiative to place us on some rows of benches a little further back, behind the closest relatives.

PAPER-THIN

You came into the church with your breath in your throat and almost climbed over benches and churchgoers to sit next to me... Haha, at least that's how I remember it when I think back on it.

A cousin of mine who has a better relationship with you didn't recognize me but came up to you and told you that, of course, you could sit at the front with your next of kin. It hurt so much, even though I know it was well-intentioned, but it was wrong. Thank you for staying next to me and telling him you would sit there.

I got a completely different response from another cousin, leading me to travel to visit her where she now lives. My cousin shared with me her memories of our grandfather's funeral. It was then, she heard that you and Dad no longer live together.

The pieces fell into place, and they understood why we all behaved strangely. She also told me how you had arrived later at the house, climbed straight up on the living room table in front of all the guests, and shouted, "Hey, I'm here!"

Epilogue

I was stunned when I heard that! Although It felt good that you took your place and took a stand.

Mum, it's pretty cool how life takes new turns and how things can happen unexpectedly in our favor. I like that you and I have a similar approach to the spiritual part of life. We send intentions, wish for things from the Cosmos, etc. Haha, well, you know what I mean. How Grandma Hilma shows us a visit sometimes, and it can get a little crazy.

I started my training as a Living Workshop Educator, which opened up a whole new world for me professionally and for my personal development, knowledge-wise, and I gained new relationships.

My classmate, now colleague and one of my best friends, proved to be a bridge to rebuilding my relationship with my cousin and you in a joyful way. We started meeting to do needlework together, and as the knitting grew, so did the relationship.

Strange how life works, that an outsider with common connections can mend family ties, isn't it!

PAPER-THIN

When the relationship was strong enough, my cousin could help me spend time with you on different crafting projects. She learned how to make jewelry with tin wire, and we continued working with beads. Crafting has always been a strong part of my life, and I'm happy to share it with you both growing up and now!

Of course, a lot has happened in 13 years.

My brother started a family, and I was faced with new situations. I also longed for a love relationship and future children...

My daughter was born in 2019. As you may remember, her father and I met at our workplace with a philosophical orientation. He worked as a special needs teacher and I handled the creative workshop in the after-school program, and I filled in as a substitute sewing teacher for grade 7.

During the three years we were together, I lived more and more like a roller coaster... Paradise could quickly turn into hell, only to swing back towards paradise the next moment...

Epilogue

It's hard to explain the turbulence and what it's like to break down through mental abuse slowly, but you were there, and you saw. But not only that, you helped me out of it.

Our daughter had turned 1, and you were babysitting while I went to get some proper closure on the destructive relationship that had gone on for far too long. I was so angry, and it all just poured out of me at the restaurant… whereupon he smiled softly and said, "You are so beautiful when you are angry."

He wanted to get back together and caught me off guard with his flattery… and I wanted nothing more than for it to work, of course… just like every other time before. A pattern that kept repeating, and once again, I fell into it out of longing, lust, and trust in the good in him.

When I didn't turn up at home as arranged, and you finally got hold of me on the phone, you could hear that we had had a few glasses of wine. I am eternally grateful for what you did next!

You packed my daughter into the pram and walked to the restaurant where we sat.

PAPER-THIN

I was happy with him close by and a party atmosphere underfoot. But deep down, I knew I was heading in the wrong direction, that this wasn't what my daughter and I needed, and that I needed help now!

I don't know what I said to my friend when I called her during my visit to the lady's room. But I explained the situation, and then I was able to walk out to you on the terrace and give you the mobile phone.

You listened, you understood, and you acted!

Mum, you took the trolley back with my daughter and gave me back the phone call with my friend, so I could get the support I needed...And you made sure the three of us got home quickly and safely, without any male company.

The road up from there has been turbulent and tough in many ways, and I am so glad and grateful that you helped us get back on our feet.

In your letter you wrote:

"My behavior towards you cannot be undone, but I wish I could do good deeds in the future.

Epilogue

I am confused about how to resolve our situation. I am unhappy about losing you.

How can we find each other again? I miss you so much, my beloved child."

Mum, I love you! You have stepped up your game several times and done so much good, not only for me but also for my daughter and your granddaughter. Watching you spend time and make memories together is so precious—something I never thought possible a few years ago.

It feels like life is just beginning somehow, and I think this book project was needed for me to land in it. When I received your letter, I had relatively recently started medication for depression, something I had tried to phase out at various stages of my life. It is only now that life feels stable and that I can, in an anchored and gradual way, step down the medication and explore who I am without the pills.

It will be so exciting, actually.

And I'm happy that you and my little family are with me on that journey!

PAPER-THIN

Many warm hugs!

/ Your daughter, Annica

This diary belongs to
Annica, 39 years old ...

First Name: Annica Maria Annci
Family Name: Vidales
Birthday: 21st of March
Zodiac Sign: Aries
Hair Color: Brown
Eye Color: Blue
Length: 160 cm
Weight: 52.5 kg

I Play the: Xylophone & Egg
Best I Know: Creativity
Worst I Know: Malicious Behaviour
Member of: Levande Verkstad
Want To Be: Highest Version of Me
Favorite Food: Vegan Sushi
Best Season: Autumn
I Fancy: My Husband

Appendix: Info about ATSUB

ATSUB, the Association of Relatives of Sexually Exploited Children has existed since 1993. Founder Birgitta Holmberg started the association when she realized how little support existed for relatives of vulnerable children in society. The support activities started with a phone in a basement and have developed into the business it is today. With a focus on supporting family members and their children, but also adolescents and young adults who have been affected.

Appendix: Info about ATSUB

Rag-doll-day is the annual event organized by ATSUB to break the silence around violence and sexual abuse of children! Instead of a minute of silence, we shout a deafening roar for all victims!

The rag doll is a symbol of the vulnerable child. All children who are vulnerable now and all adults who were once victimized as children and still bear the consequences of the abuse. A child who has been torn apart, thrown away in a corner, and forgotten about - as a thing, an object, a possession - just like a rag doll. Abandoned both by the victimizer, the child, and by society. We want to change this, join us and change it too!

About the Author

Annica Vidals is a writer and educator based in Stockholm, Sweden. With a professional background as a Teacher of Living Workshop, Annica has dedicated her career to helping people connect with themselves and others through artistic expression exercises, such as creative writing. In recent years, she has expanded her work into the digital realm, collaborating with her husband to grow their company, Online Course Secrets, which focuses on helping instructors turn their passion into profitable online courses.

This book is Annica's first published work. It draws deeply from her personal diaries, which span from her childhood to the present day, as well as the many letters she has written to herself over the years. Her love for playing with words has long been expressed through daily notes and poetry, written purely for the joy of it.

Annica's writing journey has been driven by an unwavering need to share her life story—a powerful narrative of overcoming the trauma of childhood sexual abuse and the subsequent healing process.

About the Author

Through this book, she seeks to continue her own healing and offer hope and support to others on their own paths to recovery.

Outside of writing, Annica finds joy in various creative activities, including sewing, knitting, and other forms of handcraft. She also has a passion for Swedish sign language and enjoys the process of decluttering and reflection as a means of personal growth. Annica lives with her husband and daughter in the suburbs of Stockholm, where they enjoy exploring the city together on their electric scooters.

Readers can connect with Annica by scanning the QR code included in the below.

From the publisher

Dear Reader,

If you've reached this page, you've journeyed through a story of resilience, strength, and the power of speaking out. You've read a tale of survival; perhaps it resonated with your own.

.I am Jean Dorff, author of Broken Silence and founder of The Empowering Story Program. I understand the courage it takes to share your story, for I have walked that path. I also know the healing and liberation of owning and sharing your narrative with the world.

The Empowering Story Program helps survivors of sexual abuse do just that. We believe in the power of storytelling as a tool for healing, empowerment, and inspiring others. Our motto is: 'I Tell My Story, so there is One Less Story to Tell.'

We are here to guide you through transforming your story into a published book. In 90 days or less, guaranteed, your story can be in the hands of those who need to hear it most.

From the publisher

Sharing your story is not just about you. It's about the countless others who, like you, have experienced abuse.

Your story can inspire them to break their silence, seek help, and begin their healing journey.

If you're ready to own your story of sexual abuse and publish it as a book, we're here to help.

Follow this link https://theempoweringstory.com to start your journey towards healing, empowerment, and inspiring others.

Remember, your voice matters. Your story matters. Together, we can reduce the number of untold stories.

With hope and courage,

Jean Dorff Founder and Owner

The Empowering Story website: https://theempoweringstory.com email: info@theempoweringstory.com

Made in the USA
Middletown, DE
04 November 2024

63404758R00129